Dedicated to Mary, the Mother of God; to my wife, Catherine, and daughter, Mary Ann; and to my mother, Mary Ellen, and in memory of my father, Bill.

A Catholic Perspective:
Physical Exercise and Sports

Other books by Robert Feeney

MOTHER OF THE AMERICAS

THE ROSARY: THE LITTLE SUMMA

A Catholic Perspective:
Physical Exercise and Sports

By Robert Feeney

AQUINAS
PRESS

IMPRIMATUR: ✝ Thomas J. Welsh
Bishop of Allentown
May 16, 1994

Cover picture is of Blessed Pier Giorgio Frassati

Contents

Prefatory Note

Traditionally, the Catholic Church has recognized the importance of the entire individual: mind, body, and spirit. To one living in modern secular society, however, it may seem that the development of the body has become of paramount importance. Preoccupation with the physical has led many, especially the young, to seek fulfillment through sports activities or dieting. Mr. Robert Feeney, hoping to show that "care of the body is not an end in itself, but should be directed to the intellectual and moral perfecting of the soul," (p.49) has addressed this state of affairs in his book, which is of interest to anyone concerned about the physical, mental, and spiritual well-being of the human individual.

The Catholic Church values the contribution that sports and exercise, done in proper proportion, makes to virtue. St. Paul viewed our bodies as temples of the Holy Spirit. He invited us to "fight the good fight," (1 Tim. 6:12) and visualized the Christian life as an athletic contest. He wrote, "Do you not know that in a race all the runners compete, but only one receives the prize? So run that you may attain it." (1 Cor. 9:24)

The Second Vatican Council, in the document *Gaudium et Spes*, spoke of physical exercise and sports. St. Pius X supported the reinstatement of the Olympic Games, and Pope Pius XII, known as the "friend of sports", was an avid swimmer and installed a gymnasium in the Vatican. In his teachings, he spoke of the "Sporting Ideal", that is, that the concept of sport must be understood in a healthy Christian sense. For the Christian althete, sport is not the supreme ideal, but rather must serve and tend toward that ultimate goal, so that, finally, the human individual will be able to say with St. Paul, "I have finished the race; I have redeemed my pledge; I look forward to the prize that is waiting for me, the prize I have earned. The Lord, the judge whose award never goes amiss, will grant it to me when that day comes; to me, yes, and to all those who learned to welcome His coming." (2 Tim. 4:7-8)

Mr. Feeney's book fills a need long felt by Catholic physical educators to address topics of this nature. The work is not only a compilation of Catholic teachings in the area of physical development, but it also offers guidelines for individual and family exercise programs. It addresses the need for the spiritual in every area of life, and discusses the destructiveness of the "win at all costs" mentality that afflicts so many. Given the lack of sportsmanship in so many areas of modern life, I highly recommend *A Catholic Perspective: Physical Exercise and Sports* not only for athletic directors and coaches, but also for parents and athletes.

✛ Fabian Bruskewitz
Bishop of Lincoln

Foreword

In his latest encyclical, **Veritatis Splendor,** Pope John Paul II uses a most beautiful, powerful and timely New Testament encounter between Jesus and the rich young man to teach and direct men and women of good will who are searching for answers in these modern times.

In our Western culture, especially, we are surrounded daily by a fascination and often an obsessive pursuit of self-esteem through physical accomplishments. Many young men and women use sport competitions, body building programs, weight control regimes, as well as cosmetic or plastic surgery as means to heighten their worth in today's world.

In all his writings and in so many of his public addresses, our Holy Father has consistently emphasized the dignity of the human person as created in the image and likeness of God. In addresses that the Holy Father has given to athletes on numerous occasions, he has given us a vision of sports based on the principle that the dignity of the human person is the goal and criterion of all sporting activity.

There is certainly a great deal to be gained from sports and recreational activities. Both our present Holy Father and one of his predecessors, Pope Pius XII, have touched on these values in their teachings—values such as loyalty, friendship, respect, discipline, fair play, solidarity and a spirit of cooperation.

Mr. Robert Feeney, the author of this book, has reviewed scriptural and papal teachings on the role of physical wellness and its many contributions in enhancing the quality of life. Robert Feeney has admirably captured the Church's much needed perspective on the role of athletic competition and physical exercise. The book is a treasured storehouse of Church teachings on the integration of body, mind and spirit through physical exercise and sports. His book offers a refreshing prescription for spiritual and physical fitness: "The athlete of sport uses exercise and nutrition to build up strength for the game on the field. The athlete of the spirit uses prayer to build up spiritual strength for the game of life and for achieving the final reward of eternal life with God."

This book is a must for everyone engaged in sports. I wholeheartedly encourage athletic directors, coaches and athletes to read Mr. Feeney's inspiring and informative work.

+ Anthony Cardinal Bevilacqua
Archbishop of Philadelphia

Introduction

In this book, the reader will come to understand why the Catholic Church so highly values physical exercise, sports and the contributions they make to the integral development of the human person. Research in exercise physiology and sports medicine clearly has established the need for people to be physically active in order to prevent hypokinetic disease, which is associated with a sedentary existence. This book will introduce the readers to the benefits of exercise and sports and help the readers set up an exercise program for themselves and their families.

So often today, the commercial aspect of sports, along with winning at all costs, has diminished the playing of games just for the fun, excitement or joy of play itself, along with using play as a means of rejuvenating the mind and body. In this book, the reader will be introduced to the teaching of St. Thomas Aquinas, Pius XII, and John Paul II in helping us reconstruct our view of exercise and sports as a means of perfecting the body as an instrument of the mind in the search and communication of truth. Exercise is also a means of relieving tension, and a useful way to be more patient, loving, and open to the pursuit of truth.

The readers will also be introduced to the importance of being spiritually fit recalling St. Paul's reflections on sports and exercise in his epistles in connection with striving for our imperishable reward: eternal life with God. If the sports world is to be evangelized, then there is need for theological reflection on the Christian message as it applies to sporting activity. Like the runners of old, may those who read this book hand on the burning torch to others so that the champions of sport in the future will participate with the enlightened and salutary Catholic concept of exercise and sports.

Robert Feeney

1

Exercise and Sports in the Service of the Soul

The nature of man bids us not to disconnect spiritual functions from bodily functions. An early Father of the Church, St. Irenaeus stated: "For that flesh which has been moulded is not a perfect man in itself, but the body of a man, and a part of a man. Neither is the soul itself considered apart by itself, the man; but it is the soul of a man. Neither is the spirit a man, for it is called the spirit, and not a man; but the commingling and union of all these constitutes the perfect man." [1]

Before the advent of Christianity, the Greek philosophers, Socrates, Plato and Aristotle, advocated physical fitness as a means of bringing body and soul into harmony with each other.

Long ago, it was Plato who declared: "that God, I should say, has given man the two arts, music and sports. Only incidentally do they serve soul and body. Their purpose is to tune these two elements into harmony with one another by slackening or tightening, till the proper pitch be reached." [2] Plato, in the third book of his *Republic* wrote: "Now my belief is not that the good body improves the soul but that the good soul improves the body. I believe that the teacher of both sport and music have in view chiefly the improvement of the soul."

Socrates is reported to have said, "No citizen has a right to be an amateur in the matter of physical training; it is a part of his profession as a citizen to keep himself in good condition, ready to serve his state at a moment's notice. Finally, what a disgrace it is for a man to grow old without ever seeing the beauty and strength of which his body is capable. And in all the uses of the body, it is a great importance to be in as high a state of physical efficiency as possible. Why even in the process of thinking, in which the use of the body seems to be reduced to a minimum, it is a matter of common knowledge that grave mistakes may often be traced to bad health." (Memorabilia 111-12) Aristotle had the notion that "To a good bodily constitution corresponds the nobility of the soul" (11 De Anima, lect 19). In the 5th century B.C., the Greeks spent one hour every day in the gymnasium or palestra."

The Romans did not share the Greeks' practice of physical education and sports. They were more spectators than participants. The last decades of Roman history were times of private and public extravagance. In 776 B.C., the Olympic Games were started in Greece, but were discontinued in 394 A.D. by the Christian Emperor, Theodosius, because of corrupt practices and professionalism. The moral and physical decay among the Romans were contributing factors in the fall of the Roman Empire in 476 A.D.

Physical education found no place in the schools of the Middle Ages, especially the universities. Physical education was reserved for the knights in the age of chivalry, but only for the self-protection and self-preservation needed for warfare.

During the Renaissance, the Humanists embraced physical education and sports with the same enthusiasm as the Greeks. Pope Pius II, a man of marked humanist ideas, encouraged physical exercise and sports during his papacy. He viewed the habits developed through physical fitness and sports as beneficial throughout life. St. Ignatius Loyola encouraged physical activities for physical fitness. He encouraged them to be used to build strong and healthy bodies to glorify God and to obtain greater spiritual and moral goals.

Johann Freidrich Guts Muths (1759-1839) of Germany is regarded as one of the founders of modern physical education. He wrote and had published the first manual on physical education. Not since the Greeks had anyone treated the subject of physical education more intelligently.

The Catholic Church is interested in exercise and sport because the human body is, as St. Paul states, the temple of the Holy Spirit. The Church views the body as having its part to play, like the soul, in giving homage to God. The Church prizes everything that serves the harmonious development of the human body, the masterpiece of all creation. The Church wishes to help us form a proper view of sports so that we have a healthy attitude toward competition. In this way, a sense of respect for the competitor and fair play is developed as well as for our spirit and body being trained for effort, sacrifice, brotherhood, and courtesy. The Church wishes to help us form an attitude of exercise and sports as not existing for their own sake, of their not being raised as an idol. The Church wishes to see sport transformed into an instrument for the elevation of man toward the supernatural goal to which he is called by God.

So often today we encounter people who emphasize the care of the body at the expense of leaving undeveloped the moral and spiritual aspect of human dignity. Seen in their proper context, sports and physical fitness should be in the service of the soul and service to God and others. If sport and exercise do not serve the soul and God, they are a useless movement of the body and a fleeting pleasure.

The Church values sports and exercise as virtue, if done in proper proportion. St. Thomas Aquinas wrote of the virtue of fortitude as making reason prevail over exhaustion and physical pain. One of the true values of sports and exercise is in helping one to overcome obstacles, an aspect of the virtue of fortitude.

St. Paul viewed our bodies as temples of the Holy Spirit. He encourages us to cultivate the dignity and harmony of this temple. Much of St. Paul's life reflects strength and vitality which enabled him to endure the trials of his missionary travels. St. Paul refers to sports activity to point out the spirit of courage demanded by the Christian life, a life much like a demanding sport, directing a person's energies toward the perfection of character. He invites us to "fight the good fight of faith" (1 Tim 6:12) and not to be discouraged by obstacles.

St. Paul's personality derived much from his Greek background with its emphasis on athletics. His home town of Tarsus had a stadium where games were held. It also had a gymnasium on the banks of the River Cydmus. St. Paul appears to have had a great interest in sports. He visualized the Christian life as an athletic contest and the vocabulary of athletics appear in his writings. He wrote: "Do you not know that in a race all the runners compete, but only one receives the prize. So run that you may attain it." (1 Cor 9:24) The Church values this New Testament passage as giving athletes not only motivation to win their contest, but also to win the contest of knowing the meaning of life and the purpose of our human existence, along with realizing that union with God is the ultimate victory, the eternal crown.

The Second Vatican Council in the document, *Gaudium et Spes*, spoke of physical exercise and sports as ways of helping to foster friendly relations between peoples of all classes, countries and races. The Olympic games show how sports give opportunities for encounters between people of different countries and cultures. This was witnessed at the 1992 Summer Olympics in Spain and the 1994 Winter Games in Norway.

Popes of the 20th century have actively promoted physical exercise and sports. St. Pius X supported Baron Pierre de Coubertin's attempt to revive the Olympic Games in 1896. Pope Pius XII, known as "friend of sport" was an avid swimmer and was the first pope to install a gymnasium in the Vatican. He viewed sports and exercise as ways of tempering the character and forming the will as hard as steel. Pope John XXIII gave a special papal audience to athletes from 83 nations who competed at the 1960 Summer Olympic Games held in Rome. Pope Paul VI spoke of the Olympic Games as ways of learning to confront each other in the peaceful struggles of the stadium and the court and not in the struggles of the battlefields. Pope John Paul II, an active athlete all his life, shows by his example the esteem he has for physical exercise. He had a swimming pool put in at the papal summer residence outside of Rome. He walks regularly, loves to ski, and greatly enjoys mountain climbing, which he has said in some ways evokes spiritual growth. The Pope has reaffirmed the esteem the Catholic Church bears toward physical exercise and sports as an orderly and harmonious development of the body at the service of the spirit. He views sports as a school for social education in that it encourages solidarity, brotherhood and loyalty. He sees it also as a school of human virtue, inspiring the noble ideals of courage, honesty, sense of duty, fair play, discipline, tenacity, self-control, and chivalry. He values exercise and sports as means of greater self-mastery and as a way of helping people, through basic human virtues, to develop a balanced personality. He views the dignity of the human person as the goal of sporting activity.

On April 12, 1984, John Paul II told the story of a model athlete, Pier Giorgio Frassati, whose portrait appears on the cover of this book. He was born and raised in Turin, Italy, and died at age 24. Always open to the value of sports, he was a skillful mountaineer. He always went to Mass before mountain climbing and then in the pure atmosphere of the mountains admired the magnificence of God. He was an able skier, never missing making a visit to the Blessed Sacrament after skiing. He was also fond of swimming, rowing, and bicycle riding. He had a great love for the poor and was a man of deep prayer. After becoming a member of the Third Order of St. Dominic, he prayed the Rosary three times a day. He graduated from the Polytechnic University of Turin with a degree in Engineering and was very active in student organizations. He gave time and money to help establish a Catholic daily newspaper Momento, which was based on the principles of Rerum Novarum. Pier wrote the following: "Through charity, peace is sown among people, not the peace that the world gives but the true peace that only faith in Christ can give us, making us brothers and sisters."

Pier-Giorgio was beatified by John Paul II on May 20, 1990, making him Blessed Pier-Giorgio. Many pilgrims, especially students and the young, come to his tomb. The epitaph on his tomb reads:

> At the age of twenty-four—at the very end of his university career—handsome, strong, good-humored, and beloved, he reached unexpectedly his last day on Earth; and as ever, welcomed it serenely as the most beautiful day of his life. The purity of his life and his charitable deeds bear witness to his religious faith. Death transformed him into a living standard held aloft before the eyes of Christian youth.

2

A Sound Mind in a Sound Body

A sound mind in a sound body is an ideal which can make a person worthy of the description once applied to St. Thomas Aquinas, "an orderly exposition of what a man should be, delightful to God and Man."

Sports and physical exercise can perfect the body as an instrument of the mind and help the mind in the search and communication of the truth. The Greek philosophers had notions concerning the body and soul which should not surprise us. Thought comes as a result of long preparation in which the entire body is at work. Our experience is the result of the senses and the operation of the intellect that depends on the senses. The eminent Dominican, Fr. A. G. Sertillanges wrote, "Minds can only communicate through the body. Similarly, the mind of each one of us can only communicate with truth and with itself through the body. So much so, that the change by which we pass from ignorance to knowledge must be attributed, according to St. Thomas Aquinas, directly to the body and only accidently to the intellectual part of us."[3]

Because the body effects the mind so directly, it is our responsibility to keep healthy. The early Church Father, Clement of Alexandria, in his treatise *The Instructor,* written in the early 3rd century, stated his two main concerns: keeping healthy and becoming holy. He advocated physical education and sports as worthy pursuits. Clement valued exercise as benefiting health and aiding in the wholesome development of character. He taught that one should carefully select exercises as each individual person has individual needs.

During Clement's day, the Christian Church confronted the Gnostic heresy, which had a near hatred of the body. Though we respect our bodies as temples of the Holy Spirit, we know of the weakness of the flesh due to original sin. We need health and fitness to help our soul be victorious over this weakness of our body. From the writings of St. Paul we know about the need for respecting our body: "Do you not know that your body is a temple of the Holy Spirit within you which you have from God? You are not your own; you were bought with a price. So glorify God in your body." (I Corinthians 6:19)

Aristotle and Plato stated what has come to be known as the Cathartic theory of physical activity: "that preoccupation and expenditure of energy in physical activities help to extirpate vice and direct toward constructive, rather than immoral ends."[4] Pope Paul VI seemed to echo this theory when on February 28, 1978, he spoke about how "athletic commitment provided an effective antidote to the idleness, laxity and soft living, which usually constitute the fertile ground for all sorts of vice."

St. Thomas Aquinas, known as the Common Doctor, or the Universal Teacher of the Church, drew heavily on Aristotle's world views. St. Thomas subscribed to this notion of Aristotle, "To a good bodily constitution corresponds the nobility of the soul." Aquinas considered taking care of the body as virtue and wisdom. Physical fitness and sports as means of releasing tension and bringing rest to the soul were part of the Saint's philosophy. He viewed physical education as medicine for the soul and as suitable means for refreshing and regenerating a tired mind. In book three of the *Summa Contra Gentiles*, Aquinas states that sports have a proper end, namely, that after our minds have been somewhat relaxed through them, we may be better able to do serious jobs.

St. Thomas Aquinas definitely speaks to our times since we desperately need a reconstructed view of sports and physical exercise as means for perfecting the body as an instrument of the mind and to help the mind in the search and communication of truth. Thomas speaks also to our times because of the great increase of different forms of automation; in agreement with him, we can view physical exercise as serving to help relieve tension and help restore a healthy balance of mind and body. St. Thomas's position on physical education helps us also to see the potential intellectual gains. His teaching on psychosomatic unity helps us to have a deeper appreciation for the value of physical fitness and the development of physical skills as well as the perfecting of sense experience to help us in acquiring knowledge.

As contemporary studies have shown, aerobic exercise can improve a person's intellectual capacity. Reports have shown that with exercise comes greater originality of thought and duration of concentration. Exercise increases the blood supply into the brain; and with this increase, the brain receives more oxygen with the result that many people think clearer. Attention—the nerve of study—is closely related to breathing, and for general health, we know that plenty of oxygen is a first condition.

Aerobic activity and frequent deep breathing exercises, such as slow and deep breaths, taken standing on tiptoe, are excellent means of increasing oxygen into the body, which relaxes the body and also aids in contemplation. St. Thomas Aquinas taught that contemplation is man's highest activity. There is a Dominican axiom that states: contemplate and share the fruits of your contemplation. Joseph Pieper, a German disciple of St. Thomas Aquinas, wrote a book called, *Leisure, the Basis of Culture*. In his book, Pieper writes about contemplation being man's greatest happiness.

The great English Churchman, Cardinal John Newman, saw the importance of having physical education included in a liberal education. In *The Idea of a University*, he suggested that bodily exercises are undertaken for their own sake, that they form and cultivate the intellect, rather than being pursued for utilitarian reasons.[5]

Philosopher Paul Weiss, who taught at the Catholic University of America, in *Sport: Philosophic Inquiry*, sees man's concern for excellence and his effort to perfect himself as the basic feature of sport. He viewed sport as the testimony of what man can accomplish through disciplined control of his body. The Greeks called this *arete*; when you do your personal best. In 1896, the modern Olympic games were reinstated by Baron Pierre de Coubertin with the Olympic Creed:

> The most important thing in the Olympic Games is not to win but to take part; just as the most important thing in life is not the triumph but the struggle. The essential thing is not to have conquered but to have fought well.

All the saints can be called victorious athletes of the spirit. St. Dominic was called "the holy athlete for the Christian Faith" by Dante in his work, *The Divine Comedy*. St. Dominic (1170-1221) founded the Dominican

Order in 1216. It was a time when the Albigensian heresy taught that the body was evil. St. Dominic confronted this heresy by stressing the truth of the Incarnation. He taught the Rosary, a vocal and meditative prayer to Jesus and Mary, as a means of teaching the mystery of the Incarnation. The Rosary devotion was the antidote for this false belief concerning the body.

Jansenists, Puritans, and Victorians of more recent centuries have also had an influence on the development of an unhealthy attitude toward the body, reviving in part the attitude of the Albigensians. St. Augustine wrote, "Man is to be taught, too, in what measure to love his body, so as to care for it wisely and within due limits, but no one is to be told not to desire the safety and health of his body because there is something he desires more."[6] This St. Dominic understood; this contemporary Albigensians must not forget.

3

Teachings of Pope Pius XII

Pope Pius XII was born in Rome on March 2, 1876. His pontificate lasted from March 2, 1939 to October 9, 1958. The following teachings on sports are in the form of *allocutions*, papal teaching addresses given to groups of persons.

THE SPORTING IDEAL
(Given in Rome on May 20, 1945)

Both those who accuse the Church of not caring for the body and physical culture, and those who want to restrict Her competence and activity to things described as "purely religious" and "exclusively spiritual," are far from the truth. As if the body, a creation of God like the soul to which it is united, did not have its part to play in the homage to be rendered to the Creator! "In eating, in drinking," wrote the Apostle of the Gentiles to the Corinthians, "in all that you do, do everything as for God' glory" (1 Cor. 10:31). St. Paul here is speaking of physical activity. In the phrase "in all that you do," therefore, may well be understood the care of the body, "sport"! He often speaks of sport explicitly, in fact: of races, of fights, and not in a spirit of criticism or condemnation, but as one acquainted with them, and ennobling them with his Christian conception.

In the final analysis, what is sport if not a form of education for the body? This education is closely related to morality. How then could the Church not care about it?

And in fact, the Church has always shown for the body a care and respect which materialism, with its idolatrous cult, has never manifested. Which is, after all, quite natural, considering that materialism sees in the body nought but flesh, whose strength and beauty bud and flower only to fade and die, like the grasses of the field which finish as dust of the earth. The Christian concept is very different. The human body is, in its own right, God's masterpiece in the order of visible creation. The Lord has intended that it should flourish here below and enjoy immortality in the glory of heaven. He has linked it to spirit in the unity of the human nature, to give to the soul a taste of the enchantment of the works of God's hands, to help it to see the Creator of them both in his mirror, and so to know, adore and love Him. It is not God Who made the body mortal. It was sin! But if because of sin the body, made from the clay of the earth, must one day return to dust (1 Cor. 6:19-20) God will nonetheless form it again from the dust, and recall it to life. Thus the Church respects even the body reduced to dust, because it will rise again.

But the Apostle Paul leads us on to a still nobler vision: "Surely you know that your bodies are the shrines of the Holy Spirit Who dwells in you. And He is God's gift to you, so that you are no longer your own masters. A great price was paid to ransom you; glorify God by making your bodies the shrines of His presence."

Glorify God by making your bodies the shrines of His presence! Shrines of the Holy Spirit! Do you not recognize there, beloved children, the very same words which recur time and again in the psalms? Praise God and glorify Him in His holy temple! But then it must be said of the human body too: "Domum tuam decet sanctitas, Domine"(Ps. 92:5)! Thy house must needs be holy, O Lord! we must love and cultivate the dignity, the harmony, the chaste beauty of this temple: "Domine, diligo habitaculum domus tuae, et locum tabernaculi gloriae tuae," "How well, Lord, I love Thy house in its beauty, the place where Thy own glory dwells" (Ps. 25:8).

Now what is the prime purpose and object of sport, understood in a healthy and Christian sense, if not precisely to cultivate the dignity and harmony of the human body, to develop its health, strength, agility and grace?

And let no one reprove St. Paul his bold expression: "I buffet my own body and make it my slave" (1 Cor. 9:27). For in that same passage, Paul is basing himself on the example of the keen athletes! You are well aware from personal experience that sport, undertaken with conscious moderation, fortifies the body, gives it health, makes it fresh and strong; but to achieve this work of education, it subjects the body to a rigorous discipline which dominates it and really makes it a slave: training in stamina, resistance to pain, a severe habit of continence and temperance, are all indispensable conditions to carry off the victory. Sport is an effective antidote to softness and easy living. It awakens the sense of order, and forms the man in self-examination and mastery of self, in despising danger, without either boasting or cowardice. So you see already how it goes far beyond mere physical strength, and leads man to moral strength and greatness. This is what Cicero with incomparable lucidity of style expressed when he wrote: "Exercendum...corpus et ita afficiendum est, ut obeodire consilio rationiqu possit in exsequendis negotiis et in labore tolerando." "The body should be so treated and trained as to be able to obey the counsel of wisdom and reason, whether it be a matter of work to be done or trials to be borne." From the birthplace of sport came also the proverbial phrase "fair play:" that knightly and courteous emulation which raises the spirit above meanness and deceit and the dark subterfuges of vanity and vindictiveness, and preserves it from the excesses of a closed and intransigent nationalism. Sport is the school of loyalty, of courage, of fortitude, of resolution and universal brotherhood: all natural virtues, these, but which form for the supernatural virtues a sound foundation, and prepare man to carry without weakness the weight of the greatest responsibilities.

How could we fail on this occasion to recall the example of our great Predecessor, Pius XI, who was also a master of the sport of mountaineering? Read again the description, so striking in its calm simplicity, of the night which he spent after a difficult twenty hours' climb, upon a sharp spur of rock on Mount Rosa, 4600 metres above sea level in an icy cold wind, standing up without being able to take a step in any direction, without being able to surrender for even a moment to sleep, in the center of that most grandiose of all the grandiose mountain scenery, before that the most imposing exhibition of the omnipotence and majesty of God. What physical power of resistance, what moral tenacity such behavior supposes! And what a fitting preparation those bold ventures were for the intrepid courage he would need in carrying out the formidable duties which would one day be his in facing seemingly insoluble problems, as Head of the Church.

To exhaust the body within healthy limits in order to rest the mind and prepare it for new work, to sharpen the senses in order to acquire greater intensity and penetration in the intellectual faculties, to exercise the muscles and become accustomed to effort in order to temper the character and form a will as hard and elastic as steel... that was the idea which the mountaineer priest had of sport.

How distant this idea is from vulgar materialism, for which the body is all there is of man. And how distant it is, too, from that prideful madness which cannot resist ruining the health and strength of the athlete in unhealthy exaggeration simply in order to carry off the honors in some boxing bout or competition at high speeds and which at times does not hesitate to expose his life to danger. Sport which is worthy of the name makes man courageous in the face of danger, but does not authorize his undergoing a grave risk without proportionate cause. This would be morally illicit. Pius XI wrote on this point: "When I say 'true danger' I mean a state of affairs which either by its very nature, or due to the dispositions of the person subject to it, cannot presumably be faced without some evil resulting." Hence he commented on his climb of Mount Rosa: "We did not have the least intention of attempting what is called a 'desperate gamble'! True mountaineering is not a sport for breaknecks, but is all a question of prudence, and a little courage, strength, fortitude, and love for nature and her most hidden treasures."

Thus conceived, sport is not an end in itself, but a means. As such, it is and must remain subordinated to its end, which consists in the perfect and balance formation and education of the whole man, for whom sport is an aid in the ready and joyful accomplishment of his duties: be they in his sphere of work, be they in the family.

With a lamentable reversal of the natural scale of values, some young people passionately dedicate their whole interest and activity to sports meetings and events, to training for matches, with their ideal in life being a championship...while they give only half-hearted attention to the demanding needs of their study and profession! The home becomes for them only a hotel, where like strangers they occasionally put up when passing!

Thank God that you are different, dear children! For after a fine game you return to your work with a renewed strength and vigor, and in the home you raise the spirits of the whole family with your enthusiastic description of your experiences.

Sport, which is at the service of a healthy, strong, full life, of a more fruitful activity in the fulfillment of the duties of state, can and should be also at the service of God. In fact, it encourages one in this direction by the physical strength and the moral virtues which it develops; but while the pagan subjected himself to the strict regime of sport to obtain a merely corruptible crown, the Christian subjects himself to the same with a nobler aim, for an immortal reward.

Have you ever noticed the considerable number of soldiers among the martyrs whom the Church venerates? Their body and character formed by the training inherent to the profession of arms, they were at least the equal of their comrades in their country's service, in strength, in courage; but they proved themselves to be incomparably superior to them by their readiness to fight and sacrifice themselves in the loyal service of Christ and of his Church. Animated by the same faith and by the same spirit, may you, too, be disposed to put everything in second place after your duties as Christians.

What would be the use of physical courage and boldness of character be if the Christian employed them only for earthly ends, to win some cup, or to give himself the airs of a superman? If he were unable, when necessary, to rob a half-hour of sleep or put off an appointment at the sports' ground in order to attend Sunday Mass? if he could not conquer human respect in order to practice and defend his religion? if he did not use his superiority or authority to prevent or halt with a look, a word, or a gesture, some blasphemy, evil speech, dishonesty, or to protect the younger and weaker members from provocation and suspect companionship? if he could not make a habit of concluding his sporting successes with a praise of God, Creator and Lord of nature, and of all his own faculties?

Be conscious of the fact that the greatest honor and the most holy destiny of the body is its being the dwelling of a soul which radiates moral purity and is sanctified by divine grace.

Thus, beloved sons, we have outlined the purpose of sport. Strive earnestly now to put this into practice, conscious that in the field of physical culture the Christian concept needs to receive nothing from outside, but has much to give. No less than others, you, too, can accept and adopt that which in the various sporting meetings is truly good. But in what concerns the place which sport should have in human life, for the individual, for the family and the community, the Catholic ideal is a safeguard and an enlightenment. The experience of the past decades has been most instructive in this sense: it has proved that only the Christian attitude toward sport can effectively combat false concepts and pernicious tendencies, and prevent their evil influence. In compensation, it enriches physical culture with all which tends to raise the spiritual value of man. What is more, it directs sport towards a noble exaltation of the dignity, vigor, and efficiency of life fully and strongly Christian. When he remains faithful to the tenets of his faith, the apostolate of the sportsman consists in this.

It is noticeable how very often the Apostle Paul uses sporting images to illustrate his aspostolic life and the life of struggle of the Christian on earth. This stands out particularly in the first Letter to the Corinthians. "You know well enough," he writes, "that when men run in a race, the race is for all, but the prize for one; run, then; for victory" (1 Cor. 9:24). And he goes on in a passage to which we have already referred: "Every athlete must keep all his appetites under control; and he does it to win a crown that fades, whereas ours is imperishable. So I do not run my course like a man in doubt of his goal; I do not fight my battle like a man who wastes his blows on the air. I buffet my own body, and make it my slave; or I, who have preached to others, may myself be rejected as worthless" (1 Cor. 9:25-27).

These words illumine the concept of sport with a mystical radiance. But what matters to the Apostle is the superior reality of which sport is the image and symbol: unceasing work for Christ, the restraining and subjection of the body to the immortal soul, eternal life—the prize of this struggle. For the Christian athlete and for you too, beloved sons, sport must not be the supreme ideal, the ultimate goal, but must serve and tend towards that goal. If a sporting activity is for you a recreation and stimulus which aids you in better fulfilling your duties of work and study, then it can be said that it is being used in its true sense, and is attaining its true end.

If, as well, sport is for you not only an image, but also in some way the execution of your noblest duty, if, that is to say, in your sporting activity you render your body more docile and obedient to the soul and to your moral obligations, if, furthermore, by your example you contribute to modern sporting activity a form which better corresponds to the dignity of man and the commandments of God, then you are in one and the same activity putting into effect the symbol and the thing symbolized, as St. Paul explained it. And then one day you will be able to say with the great Apostle: "I have fought the good fight; I have finished the race; I have redeemed my pledge; I look forward to the prize that is waiting for me, the prize I have earned. The Lord, the judge whose award never goes amiss, will grant it to me when that day comes; to me, yes, and to all those who learned to welcome His coming" (2 Tim. 4:7-8).

(Conclusion)

SPORT AT THE SERVICE OF THE SPIRIT
(Given in Rome on July 29, 1945)

In bidding you a cordial welcome today, we are conscious that this is an exceptional group. As directors and instructors of the Central Sports School, you represent the effort to develop man's physical powers and train his character; as graduates of many American universities, you represent the striving of man for those higher values which are recalled by the very name of the university; and finally, as a unit under military direction, you suggest the discipline by which the spiritual and the physical, the body and the soul, must be brought into harmony, the harmony of the complete man.

Sport, properly directed, develops character, makes a man courageous, a generous loser, and a gracious victor; it refines the senses, gives us intellectual penetration, steels the will to endurance. It is not merely a physical development then. Sport, rightly understood, is an occupation of the whole man, and while perfecting the body as an instrument of the mind, it also makes the mind itself a more refined instrument for the search and communication of truth and helps man to achieve that end to which all others must be subservient, the service and praise of his Creator.

It is for this reason that we must rejoice to see the direction of the Central Sports School in the hands of university men. For you will insist on the one hand on the immense help sport can give towards a man's perfecting his faculties for the struggle of life; while your academic associations will put you on your guard against the tendency, too common, alas, nowadays, of making sport an end in itself—which it can never be.

The harmony between the physical development of man on the one side, and his intellectual and moral education on the other is not easy to achieve. Hence the necessity of your instilling into your pupils the importance of discipline—not a merely external discipline, but the discipline of rigorous self-control, which is as momentous in the realm of sport as it is in that of the intellectual or moral order.

CYCLING
(Given on June 26, 1946)

We would like now to point out why the sport of racing merits special consideration, both for what it is in itself, and for its value as a symbol.

A race demands and supposes an effort, a healthy effort, a combined effort of the whole body, an effort whose power is manifested not so much by violent spurts and impulses, as in the courageous, manly, disciplined and continuous output of energy, sustained till the finishing line is reached.

But above all, how noble and resplendent is the reality of which this sport is a symbol! In the race towards eternal life and glory, you battle not to win a corruptible crown which may pass into the hands of others, but with the hope of an incorruptible crown. It is a race in which none of you run the risk of being disappointed at not gaining victory, provided that you are loyal to the rules of this sublime competition of the spirit and do not allow either tiredness or any obstacle to halt you until the goal is reached.

Go, therefore, under the radiant sunshine of Italy, of this your fatherland whose natural beauties you know and whose worthy and valorous champions you wish to be. Go, bold contestants both in the earthly race and the eternal.

LESSONS OF THE MOUNTAIN
Given on September 26, 1948)

A sentiment of devout homage has inspired you with the desire of receiving Our Blessing and encouragement on the occasion of your sixtieth National Congress. What advice could we give better suited to your character as Alpinists than this simple recommendation: learn the lessons of the mountain? It is a lesson of spiritual uplifting, a lesson more of moral than physical strength. Our intrepid Predecessor Pius XI, in recalling his past experiences as a mountaineer, used to describe them under a double aspect: the irresistible attraction of heights, and the healthy, exultant attraction of the difficulties to be overcome.

The common man likes to have his feet firmly planted on solid earth. You aspire instead to climbing ever high; on the power of your muscles, it is true...yet this yearning for altitude is in the depths of the heart the echo of a need of mind, heart, and soul. Why climb higher and higher? Why want to?

First of all, in order to see further, to look out from a better vantage point. You do not want to be like those who "cannot see the wood for the trees." As you climb up and up, the view extends further and further, the scene appears in all its splendid grandeur, the particulars melt into the whole picture and take on their right perspective. The intersecting outlines of hills and valleys, streams and rivers, combine into an harmonious unity. In the same way, too, the apparent incoherencies of life take on an harmonious unity when the action of Divine Providence is seen with a wider vision, from a higher vantage point.

Excelsior; still higher!

When the sky is clear, it lights up the earth at your feet. If the mist clothes the plain and wraps it in a mantle of darkness, you instead are up in the light, and the sea of clouds gleams snow-white below you, gilded by the light from above. In like manner, when one looks towards God, up to heaven, the sufferings and worries of this earth cannot hide the blue of changeless Christian hope, and the very uncertainties and troubles are transfigured by the rays of the eternal sun.

Still higher!

The confused, discordant noises of useless argument, or the futile nonsense of earth, the conflicts of self-love and mean interests, die out on the mountain, are lost in the majestic silence which is no whit disturbed by the soft murmurs or solemn rumbles of nature. And when the echo of thunder, or falls, or landslides rebounds from peak to peak, the heart, filled with emotion or anxiety, feels nonetheless more at ease in the midst of the purposeless and wicked chit-chat of man. Blessed is he who can dominate the worldly bustle which surrounds him, and savor in silence and recollection the peace of God.

Higher still in the cool, rare atmosphere of the mountain, the air penetrates into the remotest nooks of the lung tissue, and purges them of remnants of stale air. The heart beats more strongly, and produces a more vigorous circulation, bringing a more intense life to the whole organism. And so, too, in the calm of the spirit, in the serene breathing of prayer, the soul is elevated, purified, vivified, more free and more strong.

There comes a time, however, when the mountain seems to turn hostile. It appears then to want to protect itself or have its revenge on those who would violate its virginal solitude. It offers them nothing now. It casts them off. Sometimes it strikes them down mercilessly.

Everybody knows of the dramatic assault many times repeated by bold climbers, against the formidable Mount Everest in the Himalayas. Neither the great sufferings, nor incessant danger, nor exhaustion, nor the remembrance of those who had died, could weaken the will to begin anew.

While it is true that they hope to serve science and humanity by wresting from the altitudes their secrets, it must be admitted too that there is another force which drives them on. They are driven by a powerful interior impulse, by a mysterious passion for struggle at any cost, against difficulty, to overcome obstacles.

This tendency, when it is not shackled but guided by reason (and not by thoughtless temerity) is an aspect of the virtue of fortitude, whose role it is, according to the Angelic Doctor, to make reason prevail over exhaustion caused by physical pain: "Dacit virtus fortitudinis, ut ratio non absorbeatur a corporalibus doloribus" (*Summa Theologica, 2a2ae, q. 123, a.8).*

THE TRUE VALUE OF PHYSICAL CULTURE
(Radio Message to the Inter-American Congress of Catholic Education in Bolivia, October 6, 1948)

To counteract the exaggerated importance conceded to all that is purely technical and material, give first place always to spiritual and moral values, to the natural, and especially the supernatural values. The Church, without any doubt whatever, approves of physical culture, if it be in proper proportion. It will be in such proportion when it does not lead to worship of the body, when it is useful to strengthen the body and not to dissipate its energies, when it serves also as a recreation for the spirit and is not a cause of spiritual weakness and crudeness, when it supplies new excitements for study and for professional work and does not conduce to their abandonment or neglect or to disturbance of the peace that should reign in the sanctuary of the home.

Immoderate pursuit of pleasure and lack of moral discipline likewise seeks to invade even the ranks of Catholic youth, trying to make them forget that they bear within themselves a fallen nature weighed down with the sad legacy of original sin.

Counteract this with the education of self-control, of sacrifice and of renunciation, beginning with smaller things and gradually going on to greater ones; education of fidelity in the fulfillment of one's own duties, of sincerity, serenity, and purity, especially in the years of development into maturity.

But never forget that it is impossible to reach this goal without the powerful help of the sacraments of confession and of the most Holy Eucharist, whose supernatural educative value can never be duly appreciated.

THE SPORTING APOSTOLATE
(Given in Rome on October 13, 1948)

It gives us real and heartfelt pleasure to light the flame which will burn as a symbol of faith and prayer before the image of the Virgin of Ghisallo, a lasting sign of devotion and of trust in her maternal protection.

The flame you will receive from Our hands is entrusted to your care, that it may remain, too, as a lasting testimony of Our affectionate solicitude for you. We have already had other opportunities of manifesting these Our feelings, and of pointing out to you the true spiritual and moral significance of your sport. Today to this you add a new and precious element.

The example your champions give by their participation in sport in accordance with the enlightened and salutary Catholic concept of it, is already in itself a fruitful apostolate. But you certainly want to render this apostolate still more direct and fruitful. Like the runners of old, you will hand on the burning lamp from hand to hand. And along the length of your journey you will light from its flame other mystical flames of faith and love, which will bring into so many different places the same light and the same warmth, while you continue on your course, stopping only when you reach the feet of the Mother of God and your Mother, who in turn will lead you to the very heart of Jesus: "Per Mariam ad Jesum!"

Whilst we implore for you the powerful help of divine light and strength, now as a pledge and earnest of a generous bounty of heavenly graces, we bestow on you from Our Heart, Our Apostolic Blessing.

FUNDAMENTAL PRINCIPLES GOVERNING SPORTING ACTIVITY
(Given in Rome on November 11, 1951)

What on other occasions we have dealt with in detail, we shall summarize today in four points:

1. Sport being the care of the body, it must not degenerate into the cult of matter, becoming an end in itself. It is at the service of the whole man and, therefore, it must not only not obstruct man's intellectual and moral formation, but promote, aid, and second it.

2. Sport, in relation to professional activity, be it intellectual or manual, should provide a relief which enables man to return to work with new strength of will and nerves relaxed. It would be nonsensical and against the common good were sport to reach the stage of taking the first place in the preoccupations of the individual, so that the exercise of one's profession or trade came to be considered a bothersome interruption of the main business of life.

3. Sport should not compromise the intimacy between husband and wife, nor the holy joys of family life. Much less insistent should be its demands when the hard necessities of life already make their weight felt, consuming the energies of father, mother, and children in their daily work. Family life is too precious not to warrant this protection.

4. The same principle holds good with much more reason and with still greater importance where religious duties are concerned. On Sunday, first place must be given to God. The Church understands perfectly the need for the town dweller to go out on Sunday. She smiles with pleasure at the sight of the family, parents and children, taking their recreation together and enjoying nature as the good God has made it. Willingly she arranges for time and place for Mass. The Church does not forbid sports on Sunday. She looks upon it kindly, provided that Sunday remains the Lord's Day, the day of repose of body and soul.

EDUCATION AND SPORT
(Given in Rome on November 8, 1952)

We bid you a hearty welcome, gentlemen, gathered together, moved by a common ideal, within the Eternal

City, and brought today into Our presence by one and the same filial desire, to offer us your homage, and at the same time to renew within us the great pleasure that we always have, in being in the midst of chosen groups of specialists in every branch of knowledge having man for its object.

Your national scientific Congress, dedicated to sport and gymnastic activity, without doubt meets a need of the present time, of which your conscience has given timely warning. For you are well aware what sport and gymnastics means, especially for modern people, and how widespread is their use by all classes, how lively an interest they arouse everywhere, and what important and varied influence they have, both upon the individual and upon the community. One need only make mention of the great variety and manifold forms which sport comprises in its wide field: home gymnastics, school gymnastics, exercises with and without apparatus, running, jumping, climbing, rhythmic exercises, walking, horseback riding, skiing and other winter sports, swimming, boating, fencing, wrestling, boxing, and many others also, among them football and cycling, which are so popular nowadays.

The interest with which this immense activity is fostered and followed is shown in the Press. There is no longer any paper it can be said, that does not have its own sports page, while not a few are just so many pages devoted exclusively to this subject; not to mention the frequent broadcasts which inform the public of sporting events. Moreover, sport and gymnastics are not practised only by individuals; there are also associations for this purpose, competitions and festivals—some local, others national or international in character; and, finally, there are the revived Olympic Games, the results of which are awaited with keen anxiety by the whole world.

What purpose do men pursue in such a vast and wide-spread activity? It is the use, the development, the control—by means of man, and for the service of man—of the energies enclosed within the body; and is it the joy which comes from this power and action, not unlike that which the artist experiences when he wields and masters his instrument.

What has been the purpose of your Congress? To investigate and make clear the laws which sport and gymnastics should keep, if they are to achieve their proper end; laws which are derived from anatomy, physiology, and psychology, in line with the most recent findings of biology, medicine, and psychology, as your extensive program clearly shows.

It is your wish, furthermore, that we should add a word about the religious and moral problems which arise from gymnastics and sport, and that we should give guidance as to the norms that should regulate so important a matter.

The different purposes of sport

Here, as elsewhere, if one is to proceed to clear and accurate deductions, the following fundamental principle must be laid down: everything that serves for the achievement of a fixed purpose must draw its rule and measure from that purpose. Now sport and gymnastics have, as their immediate purpose, the education, development, and strengthening of the body in its constitution and power of movement. As their more remote purpose, you have the use made, by the soul, of the body so prepared, for the development of the interior or exterior life of the person; as their still deeper purpose, that of contributing to its perfection; and lastly, there is the supreme purpose of man as man, the goal common to every form of human activity—that of bringing man closer to God.

Having thus established the purpose of sport and gymnastics, it follows that, in these activities, approval must be given to everything which, in its proper place, helps to attain the ends indicated; on the other hand, whatever does not lead to those ends or leads away from them, or does not keep the place properly assigned to it, must be rejected.

We would now consider the concrete application of these principles. We deem it timely to consider, one by one, the principal factors that have played in gymnastics and sport, and which can be likened, as we have already shown, despite many differences, to those which are found in art. A distinction must be made between the instrument, the artist and the use of the instrument. In gymnastics and sport, the instrument is the exercise of gymnastics and sport. Let us then consider them under religious and moral aspects, so that we may see what kind of guidance may be drawn for body and soul, and for their activity in this field of sport and gymnastics.

The human body

The constitution of the human body, its structure and form, its members and functions, its instincts and energies, is clearly taught by widely different sciences, such as anatomy, physiology, psychology, and aesthetics, to mention only the most important. With every day that passes, these sciences give us new knowledge, and lead us from marvel to marvel, showing us the marvellous fabric of the body and the harmony of even its smallest parts, the inherent finality which manifests fixed tendencies, with, at the same time, a very wide capacity for adaptation. There are disclosed to us centers of static energy, together with a dynamic impulse for movement and a readiness for action. Then there is a mechanism, so fine and sensitive, of such latent power and capability of resistance, as are not met with in any of the most modern precision instruments. From the aesthetic standpoint men of artistic genius in every age, both painters and sculptors, though they have themselves recognized the unutterable fascination of the beauty and living power which nature has bestowed on the human body.

Religious and moral thought recognizes and accepts all this: but it goes even further. It teaches us to be mindful of the body's link with its first origin, and attributes to it a sacred character, of which the natural sciences and art have not, of themselves, any idea. The King of the universe, in one way or another, formed from the slime of the earth the marvellous work which is the human body. It was to be a worthy crown of creation. He breathed in its face a breath of life and so the body became the dwelling place and instrument of the soul. Thus, matter was placed at the prompt service of spirit, and the spiritual and material world were thereby brought together and united in a synthesis which is difficult for our minds fully to understand—united not only by a bond that is merely external, but in the unity of human nature. Thus raised to the honor of being the dwelling place of the spirit, the human body was ready for its dignity of being the very temple of God, with even higher prerogatives than those which are due to a building consecrated to Him. Indeed, as the Apostle plainly says, the body belongs to the Lord; our bodies are "members of Christ." "Do you not know," he exclaims, "that your members are the temple of the Holy Spirit, Who is in you, Whom you have from God, and that you are not your own?...Glorify God and bear Him in your body" (1 Cor. 6:13, 15, 19, 20).

It is indeed true, that the present condition of our mortal body makes it share in the unstable condition common to other living things, which move unerringly towards decay. However, to return to dust is not the final destiny of the human body, for we learn from the mouth of God that it will again be called to life—this time, life immortal—when the wise and mysterious design of God, unfolding like the changing succession of growth in the fields, has reached its fulfillment on earth. "What is sown in corruption (the body) rises in incorruption; what is sown in dishonor rises in glory; what is sown in weakness rises in power; what is sown in natural body rises a spiritual body" (1 Cor. 15:42-43).

Revelation thus teaches us those lofty truths concerning the human body, which natural sciences and art, of themselves, are incapable of discovering; truths which endow the body with a new value and a higher dignity, and so provide more pressing motives for us to give it the respect which it deserves. Certainly sport and gymnastics have nothing to fear from these religious and moral principles, rightly applied. Still, some forms of sport or gymnastics which fail to give that respect must be excluded.

It is sound to teach man to respect his body, but not to esteem the body more than is right. The most that is demanded is; care of the body, strengthening of the body—yes; but cult of the body, making a god of the body—no; and the same may be said of a kind of worship or race or blood, or of their supposed superiority in bodily perfection and constitution. Care of the body is not man's first anxiety, neither the earthly and mortal body as it is now, nor the glorified body made spiritual as it will be one day.

The first place in man's composite being does not belong to the body taken from the earth's slime, but to the spirit, to the spiritual soul.

No less important is the further most necessary guidance given in another passage of Scripture. St. Paul's letter to the Romans reads: "I see another law in my members, warring against the law of my mind and making me prisoner of the law of sin that is in my members" (Romans 7:23). The daily drama woven into the life of man could not be more vividly described. From the day on which their full subordination to the spirit was lost through original sin, the instincts and powers of the body have gained a mastery, and, stifling the voice of reason, can prevail over the powers of the will in striving for good.

In the intensive use and exercise of the body, this fact must be taken into account. Just as there are gymnastics and sport which, by their austerity, help to keep the instincts in check, so, too, there are other forms of sport which reawaken them either by violent pressure or by sensual allurement. Even from the aesthetic standpoint, in the pleasure derived from beauty and the admiration of rhythm in dance and gymnastics, instinct can subtly put its poison into the mind. There is, moreover, in sport and gymnastics, and in rhythm and dance, a certain nudism which is neither necessary nor proper. Not without reason did an impartial observer remark, some decades ago: "What is of interest to the masses in this regard is not the beauty of the nude, but the nudity of the beauty." The religious and moral sense places its veto on that kind of gymnastics and sport.

In a word, sport and gymnastics should not command and control, but serve and help. This is their duty, and it is in serving and helping that they find reason for their existence.

Sport in the service of the soul

What purpose would be served by the use and development of the body, of its energies, of its beauty, if it were not at the service of something noble and lasting, namely the soul? Sport which does not serve the soul is nothing more than a useless movement of the body' members, making show of something which attracts for awhile, a fleeting pleasure. In the great discourse of Capharnaum, when He wished to lift the minds of His listeners from mere materialistic ideas, and lead them to a more spiritual understanding, Jesus Christ laid down a general principle: "It is the spirit that gives life: the flesh profits nothing" (John 6:64). These divine words carry a fundamental maxim of Christian life. They apply also to sport and games. The soul is the determining and definitive factor in every external operation, just as the violin does not determine the melodies given forth from it, but needs the skillful touch of the artist, without which even the most perfect instrument must remain dumb.

In like manner, the principal and determining factor in the orderly movements of the bodily members in physical exercise, in the nimble and well-planned movements of players in games, in the powerful grip of muscles in wrestling, is not the body but the soul. Were the soul to quit the body, it would fall inert like any other inert mass. This is all the more true in that the bonds which unite body and soul are closer. In man it is a union of substances, whereby they form one nature; very different from the relationship that exists between the artist and his violin. In sport and gymnastics, therefore, as in the music of the artist, the principal, dominating element is the spirit— the soul, and not the body, which is an instrument.

Resting solidly on such principles, the moral and religious conscience demands that, in forming a right idea of sport and gymnastics, in judging the person of athletes, in paying tribute of admiration to their achievements, the observance of this hierarchy of values should be regarded as an essential norm, so that the highest merit should not be attributed to him who has the strongest and most agile muscles, but rather to him who shows the most ready ability in keeping them subject to the power of the spirit.

A second requirement in the religious and moral order, founded on the same scale of values, forbids us, in case of conflict, to sacrifice the intangible interests of the soul for the benefit of the body. Truth and righteousness, love, justice, and equity, moral integrity and natural modesty, due care of one's life and health, of one's family, of one's profession, of one's good name and true honor, must not be made secondary to sporting activities, to their victories and glory. Just as in other arts and occupations, so too, in sport, it is an unchangeable law that success is not a sure guarantee of moral righteousness.

A third requirement concerns the degree of importance to be assigned to sport among all human activities. Here, therefore, the question is not that of considering the body and soul within the limits of sport and gymnastics, but of placing these latter within the much wider frame of life, and then seeing what value should be attributed to them. By the light of natural reason, and much more under the guidance of the Christian conscience, everybody can arrive at the sure norm that the training and mastery exercised by the soul over the body, the joy, experienced in the knowledge of one's strength and in one's success in sporting events, are neither the only, nor the principal elements of human activity. They are aids and accessories to be appreciated, certainly, but they are not indispensable values of life, nor absolute moral necessities. To make gymnastics, sports, rhythm, with all their associations, the highest aim of life, would in truth be too trifling for man, whose primary greatness consists in far higher aspirations, tendencies and talents.

It is, therefore, the duty of all those devoted to sport, to preserve this proper conception of sport; not indeed to disturb or lessen the joy they derive from it, but to keep them from the danger of neglecting higher duties consonant with their dignity and respect for God and for themselves.

Exclusion from sport

We would not end this consideration without saying a word to a particular category of persons, whose numbers have, sad to say, increased since the two terrible wars that have afflicted the world; that is, to those whose sickness of body or mind makes them unable to take part in gymnastics and sport, and who, particularly in the case of the very young, bitterly feel this exclusion. While we would see the ancient adage "a sound mind in a sound body" become even more widely realized in the present generation, it is the duty of everybody to look with particular compassion on those whose lot it is not to enjoy such wellbeing. In any case, human dignity, duty known and duty done, are not limited by this adage. Many are the examples given us in present day life, in addition to those in the pages of history, which show that there is nothing to prevent a soul, not only a sound one, but sometimes a great one, even a genial and heroic soul, from being housed in a weak or impaired body.

Every man, even if he be sick and therefore unable to take part in sport of any kind, is, withal, truly a man who, physically defective though he be, is fulfilling a special and a mysterious design of Almighty God. If he embraces this sorrowful mission in a spirit of resignation, carrying out God's behest in this way, and in return, uplifted by the divine will, he will be able to tread life's way more surely along a path that is full of stones and thorns, of which not the least is that he must forego the joys of sport. His special title to nobility and greatness of spirit will be to leave to others, without envy, the enjoyment of their physical prowess and of their bodily exercise, and even to share generously in their joy; just as, on the other hand, sound and robust persons soul show clearly to the sick, in neighborly fellowship, a deep understanding and openhearted good will. The sick person "bears the burdens" of others. These latter, in the majority of cases, if not in all, undoubtedly have, together with their healthy bodies, also their cross, and they should find pleasure in placing their energies at the service of their sick brethren. "Bear one another's burdens, and so you will fulfill the law of Christ" (Gal. 6:2). "And if one member suffers anything, all the members suffer with it; or if one member glories, all the members rejoice with it" (I Cor. 12:26).

Sport in practice

A word remains to be said of sport in practice, that is, of the concrete means to be used, so that your activity may attain its purpose, keep its good name, and remove the abuses just mentioned.

All that concerns the hygienic and technical aspect, the requirements of anatomy, physiology, psychology, and the other special biological and medical sciences, are within your competence, and have been the object of your thorough discussion.

When you turn, instead, to the religious and moral aspect, the principle of finality, already mentioned, gives you the key to the solution of the problems which can arise in the forum of your conscience. In the consideration of ordinary activity, it is enough for you to bear in mind that every human action (or omission) falls under the prescriptions of the natural law, of the positive precepts of God, and of the competent human authority: a threefold law that is really only one—the Divine Will manifested in various ways. To the rich young man of the Gospel Our Lord briefly replied: "If thou wilt enter into life, keep the Commandments." And to the further question, "Which?" the Redeemer referred him to the well-known prescriptions of the Decalogue. The same can be said here. Do you wish to act rightly in gymnastics and sport? Then keep the Commandments.

Give to God in the first place the honor that is due to Him, and above all keep the Lord's day holy, since sport does not excuse us from the discharge of our religious duties. "I am the Lord thy God," Almighty God declares in the Decalogue, "thou shalt not have false gods before Me" (Exod. 20:2, 3), that is to say, not even our own body, in the physical exercises of sport; this would be a return to paganism. In like manner the Fourth Commandment, which bids us preserve the harmony that the Creator intended to reign in the bosom of the family, recalls fidelity to family obligations, which should take precedence over the so-called demands of sport and the things that pertain to it.

The divine Commandments also demand the safe-guarding of one's own life and the lives of others, as well as the health of one's own body and that of others, neither of which is it permissible, without good reason, to expose to serious danger in gymnastics and sport.

From the same source—the Commandments—comes also the force of those laws, already known to the pagan athlete, that the genuine sportsman rightly considers, in games and competitions, as inviolable. In the same way, he regards as so many points of honor: sincerity, loyalty, and nobility of spirit, by shrinking from the use of guile and deceit as he would from the stain of dishonor. He respects the good name and honor of his adversary as of equal value with his own.

Physical strain thus becomes almost an exercise of human and Christian virtue: it ought indeed to become, and be such, however great the effort required, if the exercise of sport is to rise above itself, attain one of its moral objectives, and be preserved from the errors of material-ism, which would debase its value and nobility.

Here, then, in brief, is the answer to the saying: Do you wish to make a right use of gymnastics, games and sport? If so, keep the Commandments—the Command-ments regarded objectively, in their simple and clear mean-ing.

We think that we have expounded to you the essence of what religion and moral principles have to say on the general theme of your Congress, namely, the period of adolescence and of physical activity. When the religious and moral content of sport is seen in its true light, one recognizes that this content should be inserted into man's life as an element making for balance, harmony, and perfection, and as a powerful aid in the fulfillment of his other duties.

Return again, therefore, to the enjoyment you obtain from the right use of gymnastics, sport and rhythmical exercises. Help people to gain benefit from them, so that health of body and mind may ever be increased, so that their bodies may be given new vigor in the service of the soul. Finally, and most important of all, do not forget, in the midst of the engrossing and exhilarating exercise of gymnastics and sport, what is of supreme value in life: the soul, conscience, and, beyond everything else, God.

With the fervent wish that Divine Providence will protect, ennoble and hallow sport in all its forms, we bestow from Our heart, as a pledge of fatherly affection, the Apostolic Blessing.

4

Teachings of Pope John Paul II

Pope John Paul was born in Wadowice, Poland on May 18, 1920. He was elected Pope on October 16, 1978. The following teachings on sport and exercise are in the form of allocutions given to different groups of persons.

SPORT, A SCHOOL OF HUMAN VIRTUE
(Given in Rome on August 31, 1979)

Gentlemen, beloved brothers.

While I thank you heartily for the kind and noble words just addressed to me by the President of the Italian National Olympic Committee, I express to you my sincere satisfaction at receiving you today in this house, so near the place in which your sports competitions are taking place. I am grateful to you for having requested this meeting, which is highly appreciated also on my side. Therefore, I greet you all cordially and without making distinctions, from whatever nation you come.

The XXXIII Water-skiing Championship of Europe, Africa and the Mediterranean is an excellent further opportunity for rapprochement and fraternization among different peoples. The sport you practice is certainly an extraordinary and attractive one; but beyond its competitive and even aesthetic aspects, it is always, like any other really sporting activity, a factor of human ennoblement: both in the individual sense, since it educates to a wholesome self-discipline, and in the interpersonal sense, since it promotes meeting, agreement and, in a word, mutual fellowship. And when it is practiced at the international level, then it becomes a propitious element to overcome multiple barriers, in such a way as to reveal and strengthen the unity of the human family, beyond all differences of race, culture, politics or religion.

In these times, in which, unfortunately, various forms of violence and therefore of hatred tend unhappily to rend the tissue of social solidarity, you contribute, on your side, to bearing a luminous witness of cohesion, peace and union, in a word of "getting on together." The necessary competition far from being a motive of division, is seen, on the contrary, to be a positive factor of dynamic emulation, possible only in a framework of mutual relations accepted, measured and promoted.

Precisely because your competing does not take place for the sake of mere and superficial amusement, but to give proof of your ability and of what fruits a long and arduous preparation may yield, sporting effort is a real school of true human virtue, of which the ancient biblical book of Wisdom writes: "When it is present, men imitate it, and they long for it when it has gone; and throughout all time it marches crowned in triumph, victor in the contest for prizes that are undefiled" (4:2).

In sport, in fact, virtue is victorious; and so everyone is victorious, since everyone benefits from its fruitful individual and community requirements.

At this point, I express my cordial good wishes, in view of the forthcoming Olympic games, for excellent sporting results, so that from your athletic competitions there may emerge victorious simply man, in his highest values of loyalty, mutual respect, generosity and beauty.

And from almighty and blessed God I invoke abundant graces on you all, on your families, and on your associations.

SPORT AS TRAINING GROUND FOR VIRTUE AND INSTRUMENT OF UNION AMONG PEOPLE
(Given in Rome on December 20, 1979)

Gentlemen,

It is with deep joy and sincere satisfaction that, as you wished, I talk to you this morning, Presidents of the Italian Sports Federations, gathered in Rome for the meeting of the Council of the National Olympic Committee.

While I thank your President warmly for the noble and kind words addressed to me, which illustrated well the interest of the Church in the delicate activity you carry out, I am happy to address to each of you, to the two hundred thousand leaders and the six million young people who practice in the ranks of your various federations, my cordial greeting, my good wishes, and the expression of my personal interest.

Aware of your responsibilities, which, for some of you, also reach the international level, to the rightful satisfaction of those who operate within the praiseworthy institution of CONI, I appreciate your visit all the more, because I know you are engaged at present in study of the problems connected with participation in the next Olympic Games, which we hope will be the recurrent, awaited and special occasion to confirm and highlight more and more the values of sport understood rightly and practiced serenely.

My esteem for your commitment becomes all the greater if I think that it concerns not only the preparation of athletes and programs for sporting activities of a highly competitive character, such as the ones mentioned above, but also, and mainly, the provision of adequate structures for the large youthful population of Italy, to exercise whole-some physical activity, within reach of all those who wish to avail themselves of them.

This interest of mine for your service, while it may be confirmed—as has been delicately hinted—by my personal experience and by an elective propensity, is based fundamentally on an objective examination of the values highlighted by sporting activity, as the Magisterium of my venerated Predecessors has so often emphasized in the documents and addresses.

The Church has always been interested in the problem of sport, because she prizes everything that contributes constructively to the harmonious and complete development of man, body and soul. She encourages, therefore, what aims at educating, developing and strengthening the human body, in order that it may offer a better service for the attainment of personal maturation.

The body, according to Christian concept, deserves due interest, real respect, loving and wise care, invested as it is with natural dignity, capable of a mysterious sacrality and destined to ultimate victory over death itself, as our faith teaches us. I like to repeat with St. Paul: "Glorify God in your body" (cf. 1 Cor 6:20).

Certainly, the value of the body must be supported and pursued in respect of the hierarchy of the higher moral and spiritual values, which, sometimes, require sacrifice of physical life itself, in order to affirm the absolute primacy of the spirit, of the soul, created in the likeness of God, reborn to new life by the sacrifice of Jesus Christ, the Incarnate Word, and called to the imperishable wreath, after the happy accomplishment of the earthly competition (cf. 1 Cor 9:24-25).

Practiced in this outlook, sport has in itself an important moral and educative significance: it is a training ground of virtue, a school of inner balance and outer control, an introduction to more true and lasting conquests. "Physical effort—Pius XII of venerated memory said wisely—thus becomes almost an ascesis of human and Christian virtues; such, in fact, it must become and be..., in order that the exercise of sport may transcend itself... and be preserved from materialistic deviations, which would lower its value and nobility" (To the National Scientific Congress of Sport, 8 November 1952; *Discorsi e Radiomessaggi,* XIV, p. 389).

In a social context, which is, unfortunately, in the throes of dehumanizing temptations, such as those of abuse of power and violence, feel that you are in the service of the formation of the young generation, aware—as your President eloquently expressed—that sport, because of the wholesome elements it gives value to and exalts, may become more and more a vital instrument for the moral and spiritual elevation of the human person, and, therefore, contribute to the construction of an orderly, peaceful and hard-working society.

How could I pass over in silence, furthermore, the beneficial influence that the intensification of sporting contacts with other nations can have to strengthen and develop further mutual understanding and the sense of union among peoples? It is for this reason that I look with satisfaction at the succession of peaceful competitions, such as the Olympic ones.

All these perspectives, which I have mentioned, are more than familiar to you. The few words I desired to say to you wish to emphasize the importance I attach to your effort.

Thanking you once more for this kind visit, I formulate the most heartfelt wishes that the work of your National Council may be followed by abundant and lasting fruits and, while I extend to you, to your families and to all sportsmen, cordial wishes for a Merry Christmas, I willingly impart to you my special Apostolic Blessing as a token of the gifts of divine protection.

HUMAN AND SPORTING QUALITIES
MAKE MEN BROTHERS
(Given in Rome on June 20, 1980)

On Friday, 20 June, the Holy Father received in audience the representatives of the thirty-four European football federations, belonging to UEFA, meeting in Rome for their biennial congress which took place this year at the same time as the final phase of the European Championships.

Pope John Paul II delivered the following address:

Mr. President,
I thank you heartily for the kind words you have just addressed to me, and I am happy to greet in return at the

same time as the President of the International Football Federation, the Representatives of the European Federations, gathered in Rome for their Congress on the occasion of this final phase of the championship of Europe, which is presently taking place in Italy. I bid you all, Ladies and Gentlemen, the most cordial welcome

Football, whose great competitions you organize, helping to select the players, gives every week, and in nearly all countries, the opportunity for massive gatherings, where so many families, young people—and not so young!— .find a healthy entertainment, an interest in the sporting value of the game, and even the emotion of the "fans." It is a social fact that has its importance for the millions of spectators in the stadiums, and now through television. But the importance is even greater for the players, and there I am thinking in the first place, beyond the great teams you sponsor, of the many persons who train for football, from a very early age, for the pleasure of the sport and for amateur competitions. I have been able to appreciate through experience the pleasure and interest of this sport, and I am among those who encourage it.

Values of Sport

It is not before you that I need to stress its physical and moral virtues, when it is practiced as it should be; you must be quite convinced about them. Not only does the player find, on the level of the body, the relaxation that he needs, not only does he acquire additional suppleness, skill and endurance, and strengthen his health, but he grows in energy and in the spirit of teamwork. A wholesome competition also develops team spirit and fair play with regard to the opponent, and it widens the human horizon of exchanges and meetings between cities and even at the international level. The unity of Europe, for example—I am speaking of it since you are nearly all from this continent—will not, of course, be brought about around the spherical or oval football, as its problems are set at another level, a very complex one; but sport can certainly contribute to helping the participants get to know one another better, appreciate one another, and experience a certain solidarity beyond frontiers, precisely on the common basis of their same human and sporting qualities.

Yes, like so many other sports, football can elevate man. To do so, it must naturally keep its place in personal, family, and national life, which is a relative one, in order not to lead to neglect of the other great social or religious problems; or other means of developing the values of the body, the spirit, the heart, and the soul thirsting for the absolute. The good that God wants for each one and for society is made up of a well-balanced whole.

Everyone knows very well, moreover, that the values of sport are not automatically assured. Like all human beings, they need to be purified, to be protected. Today, temptations sometimes become very strong to turn sport aside from its specifically human purpose, which is the optimum display of the gifts of the body and, therefore, of the person in a natural competition, beyond all discrimination; the loyal course of sports competitions may even be disturbed, or they may be used for other purposes, with the danger of corruption and decadence.

Great responsibilities

Those who really love sport, but also the whole of society, cannot tolerate such deviations, which are, in fact, regressions with regard to the sporting ideal and the progress of man. There again, the defence of man deserves vigilance and a noble struggle. I hope that here I concur with one of your concerns. It seems to me that that, too, in fact, is part of the framework of the responsibilities incumbent on you at the head of, or within, your European Federations.

I hope that the championships will always take place in a worthy way, in an atmosphere of joy, peace, fair play and friendship. I express my best wishes for your task, and for your teams. (There, I cannot allow myself to be partial before such well-deserving representations! So I will just say: "May the best one win!")

Nor do I forget that you are men and women who have other cares, who have, in particular, a family: may God bless your families, your children! Each of you is also, in the secrecy of his conscience, in relationship with God, who is the author of life and the purpose of our existence. The Pastor of the Church of Rome hopes, therefore, that this relationship, too, will develop, that God may be your light, your hope, and your joy. This is the meaning of the Blessing that I implore upon you, from the bottom of my heart.

For the common good

I would add a word of greeting to all of you in English. Like other sports, football passes over linguistic divisions, to express sentiments of solidarity in fair play. The immense interest of the public in this area of wholesome competition shows that many aspects of the common good are involved in the preparation and organization of the matches themselves. Through your own activities there are many opportunities to serve the total cause of human well-being. In all your contacts with the players and the spectators may you, yourselves, be sustained by the goal of service to the community and service to a fraternal Europe.

In the hope that most of you have already understood my previous words, I would just like to greet you briefly in the German language, which is also officially admitted in the European Football Federation. It is well known to me how many men in your countries are members of a football association. Yes, we can almost be sure to find in every place that has its own church, also a football field. Together with the numerous other associations of your home, this sport can build many kinds of significant ties among men, which can arouse and strengthen the feeling of solidarity in a place or district of a city.

The Catholic Church attributes great value to all such ties and elements of solidarity, provided they do not lead the individual to presumption, but make him attentive to the interests of his neighbour and direct him to constant balance of individual wishes and intentions. In this connection, my blessing willingly goes to you and your families, sportsmen and all friends of sport whom you represent.

In this meeting with the Leaders of the European Football Federations, I wish to address my cordial thought also to all football players, who are the protagonists of this sport, so popular and at the same time, so fascinating. My affectionate greeting goes to them, together with the wish that, always aware of the responsibilities they have with regard to their vast public supporters and fans, they will always give a clear example of those human and Christian virtues that must emerge from their behavior: loyalty, correctness, sincerity, honesty, respect for others, fortitude, and solidarity.

I accompany these wishes with a special Apostolic Blessing, which I extend to the members of their families and the persons particularly dear to them.

LET THE PRACTICE OF SPORTS ALWAYS PROMOTE PEACE
(Given in Rome on October 11, 1981)

Dear young athletes!

1. I am happy to welcome you and cordially greet you along with the Leaders of the Italian National Olympic Committee who have accompanied you, at the end of the national "Youth Games" competitions, to give you the opportunity to express here, also on behalf of your colleagues belonging to all the regions of Italy, the sentiments of your Christian faith and your youthful joy. I address my warm thanks to Dr. Franco Carraro, your hard-working President, for the kind words with which he has introduced this informal meeting.

2. Your presence gives me joy not only because of the spectacle of stupendous youth that you offer to my gaze, but also because of the physical and moral values you represent. Sport, in fact, even under the aspect of physical education, finds in the Church support for all its good and wholesome elements. For the Church cannot but encourage everything that serves the harmonious development of the human body, rightly considered the masterpiece of the whole of creation, not only because of its proportion, vigour and beauty, but also and especially because God has made it his dwelling and the instrument of an immortal soul, breathing into it that "breath of life" (cf. Gen 2:7) by which man is made in his image and likeness.

If we then consider the supernatural aspect, St. Paul's words are an illuminating admonition: "Do you not know that your bodies are members of Christ?...So glorify God in your body" (1 Cor 6:15; 19-20).

3. These are, beloved young people, some features of what Revelation teaches us about the greatness and dignity of the human body, created by God and redeemed by Christ. For this reason, the Church does not cease to recommend the best use of this marvellous instrument by a suitable physical education which, while it avoids on the one hand the deviations of body worship, on the other hand it trains both body and spirit for effort, courage, balance, sacrifice, nobility, brotherhood, courtesy and, in a word, fair play. If practiced in this way, sport will help you above all to become citizens who love social order and peace; it will teach you to see in sports competitions, not struggles between rivals, not factors of division, but peaceful sporting events, in which sense of respect for the competitor must never be lacking, even in the rightful effort to achieve victory.

With these thoughts and with these wishes, I very willingly impart to you, to members of your families, and to your friends, my special Apostolic Blessing, as a token of abundant heavenly graces and as a sign of my favour.

THE MOST AUTHENTIC DIMENSION OF SPORT: TO CREATE A NEW "CIVILIZATION OF LOVE"
(Given in homily at Olympic Stadium in Rome on April 12, 1984)

1. This extraordinary Holy Year would not have been complete without the witness of faith shown also by those

involved in the world of sport, that human and social phenomenon which has such importance and influence on people's way of acting and thinking today. So it is a great joy for me to be with you, men and women devoted to sport, in order to celebrate the Jubilee of the Redemption accomplished by Christ through his Passion, Death and Resurrection.

Saint Paul, who had been acquainted with the sporting world of his day, in the first *Letter to the Corinthians*, which we have just listened to, writes to those Christians living in the Greek world: "Do you not know that in a race all the runners compete, but only one receives the prize? So run that you may obtain it!" (1 Cor 9:24).

Here we see that the Apostle of the Gentiles, in order to bring the message of Christ to all peoples, drew from the concepts, images, terminologies, modes of expression, and philosophical and literary references not only of the Jewish tradition but also of Hellenic culture. And he did not hesitate to include sport among the *human values* which he used as points of support and reference for dialogue with the people of his time. Thus he recognized the fundamental *validity of sport,* considering it not just as a term of comparison to illustrate a higher ethical and aesthetic ideal but also in its intrinsic reality as a factor in the *formation of man* and as a part of his culture and his civilization.

In this way Saint Paul, continuing the teaching of Jesus, established the Christian attitude towards this as towards the other expressions of man's natural faculties such as science, learning, work, art, love and social and political commitment. Not an attitude of rejection or flight, but one of respect, esteem, even though correcting and elevating them: in a word, an attitude of *redemption.*

Positive values

2. And it is precisely this idea of Christianity accepting, adopting, perfecting and elevating human values—and thus as a hymn to life—which I would like to pass on today to you and to all those who in whatever way and in every country of the world practice or are interested in this human activity called sport.

The Jubilee sheds the light of the Redemption also on this human and social phenomenon, exalting and emphasizing its *positive values*.

We cannot ignore the fact that in this field too, unfortunately, there are certain negative or at least questionable aspects which today are rightly analyzed and criticized by experts in the study of customs and behavior, aspects which undoubtedly cause suffering to yourselves.

But we also know what great efforts have been made to ensure that the "philosophy of sport" always prevails, the key principle of which is not "sport for sport's sake" or other motives than the *dignity, freedom,* and *integral development of man!*

You yourselves, in the *Sportsmen's Manifesto* that you have launched for this Jubilee, solemnly state that "sport is at the service of man and not man at the service of sport, and therefore the dignity of the human person is the goal and criterion of all sporting activity...Sport is sincere and generous confrontation, a meeting place, a bond of solidarity and friendship...Sport can be genuine culture when the setting in which it is practiced and the experience that it brings are open and sensitive to human and universal values for the balanced development of man in all his dimensions." And you also say that sport, "by reason of its universal nature has a place on the international level as a means of brotherhood and peace," and that you wish to commit yourselves to ensuring that it "is for individuals and for the world an effective instrument of reconciliation and peace!"

Sincere fraternity

3. Yes, dear athletes, may this truly extraordinary meeting revive within you the awareness of the need to commit yourselves so that sport contributes to making *mutual love, sincere fraternity* and *authentic solidarity* penetrate society. For sport can make a valid and fruitful contribution to the peaceful co-existence of all peoples, above and beyond every discrimination of race, language and nations.

According to the *Olympic Charter* which sees sport as the occasion of "a better mutual understanding and friendship for the building of a better and more peaceful world," let your meetings be a symbolic sign for the whole of society and a prelude to that new age in which nations "shall not lift up sword against nation" (Is 2:4). Society looks to you with confidence and is grateful to you for your witness to the ideals of peaceful civil and social living together for the building up of a new civilization founded on love, solidarity, and peace.

These ideals do honor to the men and women of sport who have worked them out and proclaimed them, but in a special way they do honor to the numerous champions—some of whom are here today—who in their careers have lived and achieved these ideals with exemplary commitment!

Temple of the Spirit

4. In the passage that we have listened to, Saint Paul also emphasized the interior and spiritual significance of sport: "Every athlete exercises self-control in all things" (1 Cor 9:25). This recognizes the healthy dose of balance, self-discipline, sobriety, and therefore, in a word, of *virtue*, which is implied in the practice of sport.

To be a good sportsman, one must have honesty with oneself and with others, loyalty, moral strength (over and above physical strength), perseverance, a spirit of collaboration and sociability, generosity, broadness of outlook and attitude, and ability to live in harmony with others and to share: all these requirements belong to the *moral order*: but Saint Paul adds straight afterwards "They (namely the athletes in the Greek and Roman stadiums) do it to receive a perishable wreath (that is, an earthly, passing, fleeting glory and reward, even when it evokes the delirium of the crowd), but we an imperishable" (1 Cor 9:25).

In these words, we find the elements for outlining not only an *anthropology* but an *ethic* and also a *theology* of sport which highlights all its value.

In the first place, sport is *making good use of the body*, an effort to reaching optimum physical condition, which brings marked consequences of psychological well-being. From our Christian faith we know that, through baptism, the human person, in his or her totality and integrity of soul and body, becomes a temple of the Holy Spirit: "Do you not know that your body is a temple of the Holy Spirit within you, which you have from God? You are not your own; you were bought with a price (that is, with the blood of Christ the Redeemer). So glorify God in your body" (1 Cor 6:19-20).

Sport is *competitiveness,* a contest for winning a crown, a cup, a title, a first place. But from the Christian faith, we know that the "imperishable crown," the "eternal life" which is received from God as a gift but which is also the goal of a daily victory in the practice of virtue is much more valuable. And if there is a really important form of striving, again according to Saint Paul it is this: "But earnestly desire the higher gifts" (1 Cor 12:31), which means the gifts that best serve the growth of the Kingdom of God in yourselves and in the world!

Sport is the *joy of life, a game, a celebration* and as such it must be properly used and perhaps, today, freed from excess technical perfection and professionalism, through a recovery of its free nature, its ability to strengthen bonds of friendship, to foster dialogue and openness to others, as an expression of the *richness of being,* much more valid and to be prized than *having,* and hence far above the harsh laws of production and consumption and all other purely utilitarian and hedonistic considerations in life.

Gospel of love

5. All of this, dear friends, reaches its fullness in the *Gospel of love*, which we have heard proclaimed through the words of Jesus, quoted by Saint John, and which is summed up in the single commandment: *Love!*

Jesus insists: "Abide in my love. If you keep my commandments, you will abide in my love...

"These things I have spoken to you, that my joy may be in you, and that your joy may be full...

"This is my commandment: that you love one another as I have loved you... You are my friends if you do what I command you...

"You did not choose me, but I chose you and appointed you that you should go and bear fruit and that your fruit should abide.

"This I command you, to love one another" (Jn 15:9-17).

On an occasion as unique and significant as this meeting of ours today, I wish to pass on to all of you, and especially to the youngsters, this message, this appeal, this commandment of Christ: Love! Love one another! Abide in the love of Christ and open up your hearts to one another! This is the secret of life, and also the deepest and most authentic dimension of sport!

To all of you I wish to say further: In this age which is so marvellous and so tormented, strive to build a culture of love, a civilization of love! You can contribute to this by sport and by your whole behavior, by all the freshness of your feelings, and by all the seriousness of the discipline which sport can teach you. Live as people who stay friends and brothers and sisters even when you compete for the "crown" of an earthly victor! Shake hands, join your hearts in the solidarity of love and limitless cooperation! Recognize in yourselves, in each other, the sign of the Fatherhood of God and the fraternity in Christ!

I trust in the sincerity of your faith and your willingness; I trust in your youth; I trust in your determination to strive, beyond the world of sport, for the salvation of modern man, for the coming of those "new heavens" and that "new earth" (2 Pt 3:13) for which all of us are yearning with the ardour of Christian hope.

I feel that the Church, no less than your homelands, can count on you!

You have models to inspire you. I am thinking, for example, of Pier Giorgio Frassati, who as a modern young man open to the values of sport—he was a skillful mountaineer and able skier—but at the same time he bore a courageous witness of generosity in Christian faith and charity towards others, especially the very poor and the suffering. The Lord called him to himself at only twenty-four years of age, in August 1925, but he is still very much alive among us with his smile and his goodness, inviting his contemporaries to the love of Christ and a virtuous life. After the First World War, he wrote the following: "Through charity, peace is sown among people, not the peace that the world gives but the true peace that only faith in Christ can give us, making us brothers and sisters." These words of his, and his spiritual friendship, I leave with you as a program, so that in every part of the world you too may be messengers of the true peace of Christ!

I hope that you will walk towards the future with that "new heart" which each of you will have been able to achieve in this Jubilee of the Redemption, as a gift of grace and a victory of love!

Amen!

THE IDEALS OF SPORT PROMOTE PEACE
(Given in Rome on May 15, 1986)

Dear Friends,

1. I am pleased to meet you, the directors of the Italian Tennis Federation and the participants in *the 43rd Italian International Tennis Championship*. I gladly welcome you to the Vatican and I hope that your visit will serve as a moment of spiritual refreshment in the midst of the intense physical demands of the present Championship. I

congratulate you on the excellence of your achievements in your sport, and I express the hope that you will always consider your ability as a gift to you from God Himself.

It is always a pleasure for me to meet groups of athletes from different countries and continents. Taking part in sport and the healthy competitiveness which accompanies it embody precious values which can do much to uplift the individual, and indeed can contribute much to building a society based on mutual respect and trust, and authentic peace.

2. On various occasions, I have spoken publicly about *sport* as a real *instrument of reconciliation* in the world. Your presence here, from many countries, is an eloquent symbol of the power of sport to unite. It brings people together. Competition between athletes is a *universal language* which immediately goes beyond the frontiers of nation, race or political persuasion. All of this on condition that the men and women who engage in sport, especially on the international level, foster its inherent positive values, without allowing it to degenerate through excessive concern for merely material advantages or through undue subordination to partisan ideologies.

Yours is a very competitive sport, and the high degree of physical fitness, self-control, discipline and sacrifice which it requires can make it a truly *effective school of human and social maturity.* As a group, you are very frequently in the public eye. You therefore have a responsibility, especially to young people and children who look to you for example, to set high standards of sportsmanship and personal excellence. The ideals of fair play, honesty, friendship, collaboration and mutual respect which are so much a part of sport are very important building blocks of the *new civilization of peace* to which the youth of the world ardently aspire. I would very much like to encourage you along that path.

3. I expect you are aware that the New Testament uses the example of the athlete to illustrate a very profound aspect of human existence. Saint Paul writes: "Do you not know that in a race all the runners compete, but only one receives the prize? So run that you may attain it" (1 Cor 9:24). In a sense that is your everyday experience in tennis!

But Saint Paul is referring to *the challenge of giving ultimate meaning to life* itself. This is the challenge which stands before each individual and before humanity as a whole. Today, when there is so much loss of hope and so much confusion as to the purpose and meaning of life, cannot the values enshrined in sport open new horizons of humanism and solidarity to vast sectors of the world's young people? Is it not possible to think that leaders in various fields of sport will endeavor to give a living and convincing testimony of the beauty and worthiness of those values? Will you not put your talents and your leadership in the service of peace, of human dignity, of genuine freedom?

And in this way—to borrow another image from Saint Paul—you will *give glory to God the Creator* through your accomplishments, including your accomplishments on the sports field (cf. 1 Cor 6:20).

Dear friends, be assured of my prayers for your personal and spiritual well-being. I would ask you to take my greetings to your families and friends. And may Almighty God bless you and protect you always.

SPORTS CAN HELP SPREAD FRATERNITY AND PEACE
(Given in Rome on April 3, 1986)

1. I am delighted to be able to meet you who are participating in the Assembly of the Catholic Federation of Physical and Sports Education, which is celebrating here in Rome the seventy-fifth anniversary of its foundation.

I greet the presidents and members of the various delegations, along with the representatives of the different associations belonging to FICEP. I have noticed that almost all the countries of Europe are listed here, and this shows the vitality of the Association and its meaningful presence in the sporting environment, through the individual national organizations.

I congratulate you on the work of human and spiritual formation that you aim for in the world of sport, faithful to the institutional goals of the federation. Already in 1906 it had established its purpose of bringing together Catholic forces in order to promote healthy physical education, together with religious and moral formation. You have been faithful to this commitment, which constitutes your very reason or existence and the specific object of your apostolate. You have been faithful to your mission in past years, and you wish to continue to be faithful today, in the complex world of contemporary sports which has become a social phenomenon of great importance and interest. I wish to encourage the educational and social work carried out by all of you when you seek to propagate the true meaning of sport, not only in the world of competition and of sporting exhibitions, but likewise in the most common practice of sports: that is, in those activities that each person performs in order to increase his physical abilities and efficiency, for the good of the whole person.

2. As I already said on the occasion of the Jubilee of Athletes, the Church recognizes the fundamental dignity of sport in its intrinsic reality as a factor in human formation and as a component of man's culture and civilization (cf. *Insegnamenti*, VII-1, p. 1006). This appears increasingly true in our day, when athletic activity seems to have become a more common and even necessary reality, in fact, some demands of modern life and work, like the housing complexes of the great urban conglomerates, multiply the situations in which there is a need to find free time in order to exercise strength and dexterity, endurance and harmonious movement, so as to attain or guarantee that physical efficiency necessary to man's overall equilibrium. It is in this context that the human values of sport appear clearest. It is seen as a worthwhile way of using one's time, because in sport man acquires greater self-mastery and manifests a fitting expression of the dominion of his intelligence and will over his body. Whence arises a serene attitude of respect, esteem and redemption for sporting activity, and, as a consequence its consideration as a possible occasion of ennoblement.

May you consider your mission an important effort to bring it about that, with the proliferation of sport activity at the collective level, a "redemption," so to speak, of the sports phenomenon take place, according to the principles always proclaimed by the Church. May every athlete strive to attain, through self-mastery, those basic human virtues that constitute a balanced personality, and that likewise develop a "grateful and humble attitude towards the Giver of every good, and thus of physical health as well, in this way opening up the soul to the horizons of the faith. When practiced with wisdom and balance sport acquires an ethical and formative value, and is a valid school of virtue for life" (John Paul II, *Insegnamenti*, V-3, p. 750).

3. It must be emphasized that an authentic human and Christian formation of athletes indirectly becomes an educational instrument on a more vast social level. Modern interest in competitive sports and sports entertainment is very apparent. They take up a large part of the free time and diversion of the people of today. Obviously, we are not talking about a new phenomenon, but it is clear that today the means of social communication have made the awareness of sporting realities so universal as to make of them a paradigm of mass psychology, by exciting the emotions of the participants, and provoking emulative expressions in the spectators as a result.

Now, if sport is practiced—even in the context of competition—as an occasion for exalting the dignity of the person, it may become a vehicle of fraternity and friendship for all who are following these sporting events. One who attends an exhibition "lives" it in a certain way, participates in its spirit, feels its effects.

In these circumstances, the upper hand should not be given to the glorification of force or, even less, of the use of violence, where the sporting event becomes the occasion for the release of the latent aggressions of some individuals or groups. The spectator, too, must be capable of respecting the fundamental rule of sport as a fair and generous competition, a meeting place, a bond of solidarity.

In this regard, consider the importance of the formation of sports professionals capable in every situation of witnessing to the authentic values of healthy and proper competition. Every "champion" is in some way a model to which young people are very sensitive. Now, if a sense of equality and friendship is spread among the young, if fair relations and serene attitudes prevail in contests; if, in a word, those involved show themselves always capable of respecting the fundamental values of the human person—the end and measure of every sporting activity—then sports can help spread a more authentic spirit of brotherhood and peace among the masses of spectators as well.

4. As you see, your efforts towards an ethical formation in the sports environment appear ever more vast, valid and important. I hope that you will be able to continue effectively to carry out, with God's help, the undertaking that you have assumed as a mission.

May the paschal mystery that we are celebrating during these days be for you a motive of inspiration and hope. You, in fact, seek to assist the continual renewal of man in goodness; you seek to help him become able to direct his life towards "a living hope... an inheritance which is imperishable, undefiled, and unfading" (1 Pt 1:3-4).

With these sentiments, I wish to impart my Apostolic Blessing to all of you and your associations.

VIRTUE AND CONTEMPLATION SHOULD BE YOUR DAILY FARE
(Given in Rome on April 26, 1986)

I now greet the participants in the Assembly of Delegates of the Italian Mountain Climbing Club who are here with their General President and Central Councillors. You are all welcome to this special audience.

If it is true that sports activity, in developing and perfecting the physical and psychological potential of the person, contributes to a more complete maturity of the character, this is especially true for those who practice mountain-climbing and engage in it in respect for the ideals which this sport sustains and nourishes.

I exhort you in the words of my predecessor, Pius XII, to be "docile to the lessons of the mountain:...it is a lesson in spiritual elevation, of an energy which is more moral than physical" (Discorsi e Radiomessaggi, X pg. 219).

I congratulate you on your programs which aim at educating your members in respect for nature and in a deepened examination of the message which she imparts to the human spirit. Have special concern for the young, to train them to follow the type of life that the mountains demand of their devotes. It requires rigorous virtues in those who practice it: strict discipline and self-control, prudence, a spirit of sacrifice and dedication, care and solidarity for others. Thus we can say that mountain-climbing develops character. In fact, it would not be possible to face disinterestedly the difficulties of life on the mountains if the physical and muscular strength, which is very necessary, were not sustained by a strong will and an intelligent passion for beauty.

Help your members also to be contemplatives, to enjoy ever more deeply in their mind the message of creation. In contact with the beauties of the mountains, in the face of the spectacular grandeur of the peaks, the fields of snow and the immense landscapes, man enters into himself and discovers that the beauty of the universe shines not only in the framework of the exterior heavens, but also that of the soul that allows itself to be enlightened, and seeks to give meaning to life. From the things that it contemplates, in fact, the spirit is lifting up to God on the breath of prayer and gratitude towards the Creator.

To all of you, to the members of your club, and to all who practice the sport of mountain-climbing, I gladly impart my Blessing.

"BE EXAMPLES OF HUMAN VIRTUES"
(Given in Rome on September 2, 1987)

Dear young Athletes,

1. I thank you for this visit on the occasion of the *Athletics World Championships being held in Rome.* I am happy to meet you and welcome you in friendship, and I wish you every success in your demanding competitions.

I am happy to greet and also thank in a particular way, the Council members of the International Amateur Athletic Federation, all the members of the International Sports Organizations, the leaders, the coaches, and all the athletes from the 167 countries who are taking part in these Championships.

A special word of welcome, prompted by happy memories of meetings similar to this one, goes to the sports veterans, all the participants in past competitions, who have come to the present meeting in order to honor sport and admire the achievements of the new champions.

I also wish to greet the journalists and the representatives of the press and television, promoters of information and interest in the world of sport among people of all ages and especially among youth.

A particular word of thanks goes to Doctor Primo Nebiolo for his kind address and the gift of the gold medal of the Championships.

2. This year's meeting coincides with the seventy-fifth anniversary of the foundation of the International Amateur Athletic Federation. I would, therefore, like to express my cordial best wishes to the Federation and to commend you for your work. You aim not only to coordinate and develop athletic disciplines within the member countries, but you also strive to create, through international sports meetings, *opportunities for the fostering of friendship, brotherhood and understanding between peoples.*

The Church gives willing support to such initiatives. The Second Vatican Council observes in this regard that people are enriched with mutual understanding also "by means of physical exercise and sport, which can help...to foster friendly relations between peoples of all classes, countries, and races" (Gaudium et Spes, 61).

3. We all know that sport is a highly disciplined exercise of the human body. It seeks to develop a person's physical faculties, such as strength, stamina, skill—all working together towards a harmony of movement and action. Through sport we try to attain physical excellence, by means of necessary training and practice. Its aim is perfection in a given event, as well as the breaking of significant records, as has already happened during these competitions.

However, there is another dimension to sports activity. Sport is also an important *moment for guaranteeing the balance and total well-being of the person.* In an age that has witnessed the ever-increasing development of various forms of automation, especially in the workplace, reducing the use of physical activity, many people feel the need to find appropriate forms of physical exercise that will help to restore a healthy balance of mind and body. And from here arises that special interest and attention to sporting events, which today attract great masses to athletic competitions of every kind.

This phenomenon exposes you athletes to considerable psychological pressures because people tend to extol you as *heroes, as human models* who inspire ideals of life and action, especially among youth. And this fact places you at the center of a particular social and ethical problem. You are observed by many people and expected to be outstanding figures not only during athletic competitions but also when you are off the sport field. You are asked to be *examples of human virtue,* apart from your accomplishments of physical strength and endurance.

4. For this reason there are *certain values* in your life which cannot be forgotten. These values will set you on that clear track which has to be followed in order for you to reach life's ultimate goal.

Primary among them is the *religious meaning of human existence.* Sport, as you well know, is an activity that involves more than the movement of the body; it demands the use of intelligence and the disciplining of the will. It reveals, in other words, the wonderful structure of the human person created by God as *spiritual being,* a unity of body and spirit. Athletic activity can help every man and woman to recall that moment when God the Creator gave origin to the human person, the masterpiece of his creative work. As the Scriptures tell us: "Then the Lord God formed man of dust from the ground, and breathed into his nostrils the breath of life; and man became a living being" (Gen 2:7). We are reminded then that even the laws of sport belong to a certain order, which is basically that of all creation. The observance of this order is the condition for success.

May this truth never be overlooked or set aside in the world of sport, but may it always shine forth clearly. For athletic activity is never separated from the activities of the spirit.

If sport is reduced to the cult of the human body, forgetting the primacy of the spirit or if it were to hinder your moral and intellectual development, or result in your serving less than noble aims, then it would lose its true significance and, in the long run, it would become even harmful to your healthy and full growth as human persons. You are *true athletes* when you prepare yourselves not only by training your bodies but also by constantly engaging the spiritual dimensions of your person for a *harmonious development of all your human talents.*

5. My prayer for you, young athletes, is that you will always grow in respect for the authentically human values of sport, thanking God the Creator who has endowed you with extraordinary talents—talents that can be used to work for true peace and fraternal understanding among all peoples of the world.

May your meeting in these days serve this worthy aim. I entrust to the Lord all your noblest hopes and aspirations and I invoke divine blessings upon you, your families and all the persons who are dear to you.

5

Benefits of Exercise

Long ago, Hippocrates said, "Exercise strengthens while inactivity wastes." Hypokinetic diseases, which refer to a disease or condition related to or caused by a lack of regular physical exercise, are all too prevalent today. Heart diseases account for nearly one-half of all deaths in the U.S. The United States has the highest death rate from cardiovascular disease of any nation in the world. Hans Kraus, M.D. and Kenneth Cooper, M.D., have in their medical careers demonstrated how exercise and sports can help in the prevention of hypokinetic disease.

1. Aerobic exercise, such as brisk walking, running, swimming, bicycle riding, done continually for at least 20 minutes, strengthens the heart, the pump of life.

The heart is a muscle that beats on the average of 72 beats a minute, and 100,000 beats a day, circulating 2,000 gallons of blood a day through 60,000 miles of blood vessels.

Exercise increases the size and strength of the heart. It increases the total blood volume being pumped per beat to the cells of the body. It also causes a reduction in the resting heart rate. This slower heart rate and increased stroke volume creates a greater rest for the heart between beats. Studies have shown that people who exercise have a lower resting blood pressure than people who do not exercise. Exercise lowers the concentration of fat in the blood which can block the coronary arteries, which then can cause a heart attack. Another benefit of exercise for the heart is that it enlarges blood vessels and also increases the number of red blood cells, thereby increasing the capacity to carry oxygen to the cells of the body.

2. Aerobic exercise increases the amount of oxygen we take into our system.

The smallest unit of the body is the cell; groups of cells joined together are called tissues and combinations of different kinds of tissues form organs. Each of the cells of our body needs a sufficient supply of oxygen. We need energy in all the processes of life, and this needed energy is produced in the cells by chemical reactions which consume oxygen. Oxygen being supplied to body tissues is the basis of conditioning. We need oxygen for our heart, brain and other organs. We can live for weeks without food, but hardly five to twelve minutes without oxygen. Muscles burn energy and call on the heart and lungs to deliver oxygen-rich blood to them. This same blood returns with carbon dioxide which it expels into the lungs. A muscle without a proper oxygen supply will contract a few hundred times before starting to fatigue.

We get oxygen from the lungs, which receives it from the air we breathe. We assimilate about 21 percent oxygen from the air we breathe. Ernst Van Aaken, M.D., in his work on sports medicine and physical fitness, has demonstrated that while sedentary we take in 6-10 liters of air per minute with 12-20 breaths assimilating one-quarter of a liter of oxygen per minute from this air. In endurance exercise, such as light running or bicycle riding, done continuously for a half hour and at a heart rate of between 130-150 beats per minute, we assimilate 2-3 liters of oxygen per minute from the 50-60 liters of air that we breathe in. Dr. Van Aaken encourages endurance activity that at a minimum causes us to assimilate 1½-2 liters of oxygen per minute.

Another benefit of exercise is that it increases the rate at which enzymes in the muscles pick up oxygen from the blood. Exercise also strengthens the intercostal muscles (located between the ribs). The increased strength of the intercostal muscles increases the size of the chest cavity, allowing more air to enter into the lungs with each breath, thus increasing our oxygen supply.

3. Exercise relieves tension from muscles and helps us to relax.

In our everyday life, we are affected by many interior and exterior irritations and annoyances—personal problems, traffic jams, the ring of the telephone, the loud noises of the radio or television. When our bodies get ready to respond to an irritation or a challenge, our muscles get tense, adrenaline pours into our system, our heart beats faster, we breathe quicker, and our blood pressure rises.

Underexercised muscles never get a change to get rid of tension. A muscle shortens with tension and this tension prohibits muscular relaxation. A muscle must relax, as it is part of its function, and if it does not relax, it stays tight. With activity, there are small changes in the electrical activity within the muscle. Electromyographic (EMG) instruments can indicate levels of nervous tension by measuring the degree of electrical changes in the muscle, the principle being that the more electrical impulses in the muscles, the higher the tension level is. Studies have shown that after exercise, the electrical activity in the muscles is lower. Aerobic and therapeutic exercises release tension making the muscles more flexible and resilient.

The increased amount of adrenaline in the blood due to constant irritation tends to tighten and restrict muscles of the body. Vigorous exercise can help break excess adrenaline and lessen the detrimental effects of adrenaline produced by emotional stress. Many psychiatrists recommend physical activity and sports for tension relief. Many of them believe that exercise and sports serve better than the pills as a tranquilizer for the release of tension. Ronald M. Lawrence, M.D., Ph.D., a psychiatrist, noted in the field of sports medicine and physical fitness, asserts that as you do aerobic exercise your brain produces endorphins, a hormone that helps in relieving nervous tension and aids in relaxation. William Menninger, M.D., a psychiatrist and founder of the Menninger Clinic in Topeka, Kansas, encouraged physical activity as an outlet for instinctive aggressive drives by enabling a person to "blow off steam," thus providing relaxation and being a supplement for daily work.

4. Aerobic exercise provides psychological benefits.

Many reports have indicated that as you exercise, you bring in more oxygen into your brain and this makes you more alert and attentive. Ray Killinger, M.D., a psychiatrist, in his report on aerobic exercise has indicated that "aerobic fitness results in improvement in the following categories of the thinking process: originality of thought;

duration of concentration; mental response time; ability to change topics and subjects quickly; depth of thinking, duality of thought—the ability to entertain a number of ideas at once; and finally, mental tenacity."[7]

Kenneth Cooper, M.D., M. Ph., of the Aerobics Center in Dallas, Texas, is convinced that being physically fit can definitely help in being psychologically fit. In studies conducted at his Clinic and Institute for Aerobic Research, exercise has shown to help people better able to handle stress, gain in feelings of well-being, and help in reducing depression. Dr. Cooper attests to the conviction that aerobic exercise helps people in improving their self-image, and along with improved self-image, become more confident and outgoing.

Robert S. Brown, M.D., a psychiatrist at the University of Virginia, and Keith Johnsgard, Ph.D., author of the book, *The Exercise Prescription for Depression and Anxiety*, both believe that running, brisk walking, swimming and bicycling may definitely be the best prescription for mild depression. Dr. Brown finds that aerobic exercise works better than pills in controlling moderate depression. Dr. Malcolm Carruthers and a medical team from England reported that as little as 10 minutes of endurance exercise can double the body's level of norepinephrine, a neurohormone that is associated with alertness and feeling joyous. Researchers claim that stress lowers norepinephrine levels in the brain, whereas, exercise tends to increase norepinephrine in the brain. Depressed people are known to be low in norepinephrine.

As you do aerobic exercise, your brain produces endorphins, which are morphine-like substances which are produced by the brain and pituitary gland that aids the body in resisting pain. Ronald M. Lawrence, M.D., Ph.D., a psychiatrist at the UCLA Neuropsychiatric Institute and noted in the field of sports medicine and physical fitness, asserts that "endorphins help you learn and remember, counteract depression; relax you and relieve nervous tension and makes it easier for you to sleep soundly at night."[8] Dr. Lawrence asserts that "the more you exercise, the more endorphins you manufacture and the better you feel."[9] He thinks that endorphins could be the source of the "runners high" that runners talk about.

In all the literature that pertains to the psychological benefits of exercise, there is a consensus that exercise does produce an improved sense of well-being. This sense of well-being is attributed to such things as a decrease in anxiety, stress and depression, a more positive body image and self-esteem and more energy. Literature in this area also attests to the ancient Greek notion that a sound body ensures a sound mind.

5. Exercise helps to control obesity.

Obesity has become a problem for many in the United States in the past few decades. Regular exercise, especially aerobic exercise, is one of the keys to losing excess body fat, increasing lean body mass, and in maintaining a balanced metabolism.

Aerobic exercise raises your basal or resting metabolic rate for between six and eighteen hours, so you will continue to burn extra calories long after you finish your exercise, even when you are sleeping. Aerobic exercise and restriction of caloric intake reduces fat; whereas, people who go on a diet without exercise tend to often lose muscle tissue and if they do lose fat, they usually regain it after the diet is over. Exercise not only burns fat but also tones and firms muscles.

Exercise can help burn up more calories than you take in and this can help lose excess fat. In most cases, inactivity is the cause of obesity. Harvard's Dr. Jean Mayer, well known scientist and nutritionist, has stated that he is "convinced that inactivity is the most important factor explaining the frequency of creeping overweight in modern societies."[10]

Even though we need a certain percentage of fat, excess fat can lead to diseases such as diabetes, coronary artery disease, and high blood pressure. In general, men should try to keep their fat weight at less than 16 to 19 percent of their total body weight; whereas, women should maintain it at under 22 percent. An expert would evaluate a subject's physique by measuring skin-fold thickness with calipers, or by the more exact method of hydrostatic underwater weighing.

Aerobic exercise gives the muscles time to burn off fat; whereas, burst of energy called anaerobic exercise tends to burn glucose for fuel instead of fat. The areas of the body you should see a decrease in body fat are: abdomen, thighs, buttocks and hips. Research has found that swimming does not produce the desired effect of losing body fat. It is better to do the aerobic exercises such as running, bicycle riding, stationary bike, cross-country skiing or brisk walking. Sit-ups done for losing body fat in the abdomen does not produce the desired effect.

Exercise is used to change muscle chemistry so that we burn fat more efficiently. Covert Baily, author of *Fit or Fat*, asserts that aerobic exercise produces a growth of fat burning enzymes in your muscles. He recommends that aerobic exercise be done continuously for at least 12 minutes at a pace that enables you to go as fast as you can without getting out of breath and without feeling exhausted when you finish. He recommends a heart rate 60 to 85% of your maximum heart rate while you exercise (more on heart rate and target zone in Chapter 6). Studies have found that vigorous continuous aerobic exercise tends to reduce the appetite and that is why some fitness experts recommend brisk walking, running, stationary bike or bicycling before dinner.

6. *Exercise, depending on the type, increases size, strength and endurance of the muscles.*

Aerobic exercise, become of the efficient delivery of oxygen and removal of waste products, increases the endurance of muscles allowing them to work longer without getting fatigued. Weight training and calisthenics causes an increase of strength in the muscles due to a thickening of the sarcolemma of the muscle fibers. The amount of connective tissue within the muscle also thickens. The size of the muscle fibers are increased due to exercise. Exercise also causes an increased blood flow into the muscle tissue resulting in an increase in the size of the muscle. Exercise causes an increase of capillaries, thus, providing better circulation of blood to the muscle.

7. *Vigorous exercise makes your bones grow in size, thickness and strength.*

There are 206 bones in the normal adult body. Aerobic exercise and other exercise that moves your body against gravity makes bones grow in size, thickness and strength. Exercise can protect people against bone deterioration known as osteoporosis. Brisk walking is excellent for the hips and spine.

8. Exercise is also known to keep the digestive and excretory organs in good shape.

Exercise helps the muscles and nerves of the stomach and intestines become well toned and improves their ability to work in an efficient manner.

6

Guidelines for an Individual and Family Exercise Program

The foundation for an individual exercise program is a medical evaluation so as to obtain clearance for a program of exercises. Adults and even the young would be wise to invest in a medical evaluation prior to participating in competitive sports. An exercise prescription which provides the proper dosage should be given according to an individual's age, level of fitness, ability, disability, likes and dislikes. As early as the 3rd century, Clement of Alexandria, a Church Father whose main concerns were keeping healthy and becoming holy, taught that one should carefully select exercises as each individual person has different needs. A professionally trained expert such as an exercise physiologist, physical education teacher, physical therapist, or a sports medicine professional can help with an individualized prescription of exercise. This help can prevent problems that arise when people do not recognize their own limitations, thereby going beyond a safe level of exercise.

When we think of exercise in terms of prescription and proper dosage, we remember St. Thomas Aquinas' view of exercise as medicine for the soul and regeneration for the fatigued mind.

Parents need to be concerned with their childrens' aerobic fitness. The 1987 National Children and Youth Fitness study reported that one-third of all youth, 10-18, did not exercise enough to give them any aerobic health-related benefits. A study sponsored by the AAU and Chrysler Corporation found that only 32 percent of children ages 6 to 17 meet minimal standards for cardiovascular fitness, flexibility, upper body strength, and abdominal strength.

The Fathers of the Second Vatican Council stressed the role of parents as the primary educators of their children. It is best for parents to start out by being examples of fitness for their children, and by giving them opportunities to improve their fitness and motor skills so as to achieve a level of athletic achievement according to their developmental age and interest. Children need to be offered opportunities that will develop their health and character instead of being offered television and video games as after school activities. Family fitness activities that are fun and enjoyable can be helpful in improving communication between family members.

EXERCISE PRESCRIPTION

When considering a program of exercise, attention should be given to 1) type of activity, 2) intensity of activity, 3) duration and frequency of activity.

TYPES OF ACTIVITY

Individuals or families should select activities and exercises that they enjoy and ones that are suited to their present fitness level. It is important to gradually get in shape, adapting your body to regular exercise. It is best to view exercise and sports as a lifetime project; one that will need our perseverance and motivation. Pope John Paul II has remarked that individuals who care for their body and make good use of the body through exercise and sports will benefit from the marked consequences of psychological well-being. He has also remarked that we can develop through long hours of exercise and effort the power of concentration and the habit of discipline.

An exercise program should place primary emphasis on aerobic exercise that is undertaken for health-related benefits. Muscular strength, muscular endurance, and flexibility are also important and should be integrated into one's exercise program. Aerobic exercise develops cardiorespiratory endurance. The word *aerobic* is derived from two Greek words meaning "life" and "air." Activities that increase fresh supplies of oxygen and done for prolonged periods (at least 20 minutes) are called aerobic. We develop endurance and a strong will through these activities. Pope Pius XII viewed exercise as ways of tempering the character and forming the will as hard as steel.

As far as aerobic activities for children under 10 are concerned, it is recommended that parents emphasize aerobic play such as: tag, chase, hide and seek, and random running instead of the regular 20 minutes or more of the continuous vigorous activity. (An excellent resource book for aerobic play for children and family fitness activities is *The Family Fitness Handbook* by Bob Glover and Jack Shepherd, Penguin Books, 1989.)

Aerobic activities that use large muscle groups that are rhythmical and maintained continuously are:

Brisk walking: Walking is a natural exercise, one that is recommended for beginners, for those who have not exercised for some time, and even for the fittest. Walking is nonjarring, making it more unlikely of injuring yourself. Besides aerobic and weight control benefits, people who start their exercise program with walking tend to stick with it and not give up. Walking is known to be an excellent way to build strong bones and help prevent osteoporosis.

For those who have been sedentary, it is best to begin with a 10 minute walk, then add 5 minutes to your walk until you are walking for 30-45 minutes per outing. For some, walking is a way of preparing for more vigorous activity such as jogging, biking and swimming. For others, they are content for walking to be their main exercise activity. Good shoes are essential for walking. Running shoes or shoes designed for exercise walking are recommended.

We read of the saints of the Middle Ages being great walkers, walking across Europe; especially St. Dominic, the great preacher of the Rosary, described by his contemporaries as the "strong athlete." His vigorous nature and physical energy, aided by God's grace, strengthened him to be morally fit and robust in the interior, spiritual life.

Jogging/Running: For beginners, for those who are sedentary, out of shape, or overweight, they should use walking as the primary means of getting in shape before they begin jogging or running. When you do start jogging, start out walking for 5 minutes, then a slow jog for 5 minutes, alternating these two movements. This can be done for the first 3-4 weeks until you can comfortably jog without discomfort. Observing good running form is essential. Keep hands and shoulders relaxed, head up, and make sure you do not run on the balls of your feet, but more of a flat-footed foot strike. Good running shoes are crucial. If you have a history of orthopedic problems or health problems, or have been sedentary for some time, it is best to seek medical clearance before starting a running routine.

Swimming: Swimming is the second most popular sport in America. As well as the aerobic benefits, swimming is excellent for developing muscle strength and muscle endurance. It puts less stress on the joints, ligaments, and tendons than do other activities due to the natural buoyancy of water.

It is important to learn how to swim efficiently using different strokes and in learning to breathe properly. The crawl (or free style), backstroke, breaststroke, and sidestroke are great for developing your shoulder, chest, back, leg and arm muscles. The sidestroke is great for warming up and for slowing and cooling down. It is best to gradually work up to doing continuous laps by taking rests as needed between laps. Many recommend getting in shape by walking or riding a stationary bike before taking on a swimming routine, and as with other activities, medical clearance is advised. Pope Pius XII was an avid swimmer. Pope John Paul II is known to be very fond of swimming.

Cycling: Outdoor recreational cycling is an excellent means of aerobic conditioning and weight loss. Because of the bike seat supporting much of your weight, there is less stress on your joints than in jogging or running. For beginners, those out of shape, it is best to build up gradually, perhaps 10 minutes a day, then adding on 5 minutes per week. Be sure to pedal with the balls of your feet, not your insteps or heels. It is important to find the right seat height, if you want to avoid knee pain. This is done by sitting on the seat with your legs extended and the ball of your foot resting on the pedal at the bottom of the pedal stroke position. There should only be a slight bend (10-15 degrees) in the knee - adjust your seat accordingly. The indoor stationary bike is also an excellent way of exercising. It is great for when it is too wet or too hot outside. You get the same benefits as from outdoor cycling except for the scenery, sunshine and fresh air. Be sure you check the proper seat height as you do with outdoor cycling. It is advised to get medical clearance if you have health problems, or are really out of shape, before taking on cycling.

Excellent resource books for aerobic activities and fitness are: *The Aerobics Way* by Kenneth Cooper, M.D., M.Ph. (M. Evans and Company, Inc.) and *The Aerobics Program for Total Well-Being* by Kenneth Cooper, M.D., M.Ph. (Bantam Books).

Musculoskeletal conditioning activities that develop muscular strength and endurance are:

Calisthenics: These are isotonic exercises that use our own body weight for resistance. Muscular fitness involves two health-related components: strength and muscular endurance. Strength helps in doing more work at one time, to move more easily and in developing good posture. Muscular endurance helps you to keep on working at a given activity. Children are very deficient in both these areas. Calisthenics can help develop both components. They can also help us in resisting fatigue, prevent back problems, and help in enjoying recreational and sport activities without injury. Children seven years old or under are recommended to use playgroup apparatus to develop strength and endurance. For minimal fitness, 3 days a week is encouraged. Two basic calisthenics are push-ups and sit-ups.

Push-ups: These are excellent for developing strength and endurance in the upper body. A study by the American Athletic Union in 1987 found that 40 percent of boys and 70 percent of girls can do only one push-up.

Procedure: The recommended way of doing a push-up is to lie on your stomach on the floor with your hands palms down on the ground about shoulder width apart. With your toes on the ground and your back and legs straight, push slowly upward until arms are fully extended, then lower yourself to the ground. Gradually work yourself up to doing 10 to 20 push-ups for minimal fitness. You can then try doing 2 or 3 sets of 10-20 push-ups each with rests between sets. Youngsters and adults who are beginners are recommended to start off with modified push-ups. These are done the same way except that you keep your knees on the ground. Be sure you do not hyperextend your back—keep your back straight.

Sit-ups: These are excellent for developing abdominal muscles. Low back pain is a major problem in the U.S. It is reported that 80 percent of low back problems result from lack of flexibility in the back and hamstring muscles, and poor posture, which results from weak abdominal muscles. Strong stomach muscles can help prevent the forward tilt of the pelvis, which can cause pain. Dr. Hans Kraus, author of the book, *Hypokinetic Disease*, reported that 25 percent of all U. S. youngsters cannot do a single sit-up because of weak abdominal muscles.

Procedure: The proper way of doing a sit-up is to lie on your back with knees bent with your heels about 15 inches from the buttocks. Cross your arms in front of your chest with hands holding opposite shoulders. Raise yourself off the ground until your elbows touch your thighs, then return to the ground. For minimal fitness, gradually work up to 10-20 sit-ups. Another recommended way is to lie on your back with knees bent, reach for the top of your knees, lifting your shoulder blades off the ground. Hold for 10 seconds. Repeat and gradually work up to 10-20 times. You can also do the same but roll your shoulders and push your right hand against the outside of the left knee, return and then raise your left hand against the outside of the right knee. This way helps develop the oblique muscles on each side of the abdomen.

Weight training: This is the use of free weights such as dumbbells, barbells, and exercise machines. Exercise machines that are most used are Universal Gym and Nautilus. It is recommended that children under 13 not use weight training but calisthenics to develop strength and endurance. The principle for weight training is that for strength you lift heavy weight a few times; whereas, for endurance, you lift lighter weights a greater number of times. It is most important to receive proper instruction so as to learn proper safety measures and proper techniques before engaging in a weight training program. Teenagers who use weight training are encouraged to be under adult supervision. Three days a week, every other day is the recommended frequency for weight training. (A good resource book for weight training and fitness is *Sensible Fitness* by Jack H. Wilmore, Ph.D., Leisure Press.)

Recreational and sports activities do offer exercise but a good principle to remember is: do not play sports to get in shape, but get in shape to play sports.

Most sports have more to do with offering skill-related fitness than health-related fitness. Popular games such as baseball, basketball, football, tennis, racquetball, and golf, although they are fun, are stop and go and therefore, offer less aerobic benefits than continuous and rhythmic movement that involves large muscle groups. Games that consist of quick movement and short bursts of speed are not as beneficial for cardiovascular fitness.

There is a great deal to be gained from sports and recreational activities, values that Pope Pius XII and Pope John Paul II have touched on in their teachings; values such as loyalty, friendship, respect, discipline, fair play, solidarity, and a spirit of cooperation.

The American Academy of Pediatrics recommends that children do not engage in team sports before the age of 6. Some other medical experts and physical education professionals do not recommend intense athletic competition before the age of 10. They state that activities should not be used in comparing performance between children, but should emphasize learning basic skills and socialization and just having plain fun. They recommend starting with swimming, biking, and running activities as ways of moving into team sports.

Parents should teach their children at an early age locomotor skills such as running, skipping, jumping, hopping, galloping, and balancing. Manipulative skills such as throwing, catching, kicking, dribbling, and rolling a ball should also be taught. These are all sports-related skills that can help their children later on in athletic achievements according to their developmental age and likes. It is important that fathers and mothers exercise and play with their children and organize family games, hikes and walks. (A good resource book for locomotor and non-locomotor skills and elementary physical education information is: *Dynamic Physical Education for Elementary School Children* by Victor P. Dauer and Robert P. Pangrazi, Burgess Publishing Co.)

INTENSITY

It is important to maintain a sufficiently high heart rate while exercising so that you achieve a "training effect." The target heart rate is the rate at which your heart should be beating so that you achieve the maximum aerobic conditioning effect. There is a target heart rate zone that can be determined so as to help you determine what intensity you should maintain during exercise. It is determined by first calculating your maximum heart rate. There are several accepted formulas for arriving at your maximum heart rate; one is—

[220 minus your age = maximum heart rate]

You then calculate your target heart rate by using a percentage formula of your maximum heart rate. Some recommend 60 percent to 70 percent of your maximum heart rate for people who have been sedentary for some time. Others recommend 65 to 80 percent of your maximum heart rate as an overall formula. So to find out your target heart rate zone, you would multiply 0.65 times your maximum heart rate, then multiply 0.80 times your maximum heart rate to determine the range at which you should maintain your heart rate per minute during exercise. Let's say you are 40-years-old—your maximum heart rate is 220-40 = 180. You then multiply 180 x 0.65 = 117, then 180 x 0.80 = 144. So, the range in which you should exercise is 117-144. You can monitor your heart rate during exercise and immediately after exercise by taking your pulse with the tips of two fingers on the radial artery (on the inside of your wrist below the base of your thumb), or pressing lightly on the carotid artery of your neck (on either side of the Adam's apple) with index and middle fingers. You then use a watch and count your pulse for 15 seconds and then multiply by 4 to arrive at your heart rate per minute. You can also use the talk test instead of taking your pulse. Basically, this is listening to your body and exercising at a rate where you can carry on a regular conversation during exercise; if you get out of breath and cannot talk in a regular fashion, you are exercising too fast. The key is to take it gradually. Know your limits and do not push yourself beyond your limits. Generally, adults need 8 to 10 weeks to get into fairly good shape after being sedentary.

If you gradually adapt your body to regular exercise, you lessen your chances of injury and discouragement. Start off at the lower range of your target zone until you think your fitness has improved and then gradually move on to the upper range.

FREQUENCY AND DURATION

To build cardiovascular fitness, it is recommended that you exercise 3-5 days per week. The time of exercise refers to your activity that is maintained within your target heart rate zone. This does not include warm-up and cool down. Beginners are recommended to start off with 10-20 minutes of aerobic activity. Those in average and good shape are recommended to do 20-30 minutes of aerobic activity. Children around ages 6-9 should limit their activity to 10-20 minutes of imaginative aerobic activity. Beginners are recommended to limit themselves to short periods of vigorous exercise, mixed with moderate levels. Many people start their time with walking. They are more likely not to get injured and stay with their program than with people who start with vigorous exercise. Remember sore muscles are inevitable in the beginning but this will lessen with regular exercise.

After medical clearance has been obtained and the exercise prescription taken into consideration, a total exercise program should include: 1) a warm-up and stretching period, 2) the aerobic conditioning period, 3) the cool down.

The warm-up and stretching period: This is a 5 to 10 minute period used to gradually prepare your body with low level activity for the more vigorous aerobic activity that follows. This low level activity includes static stretching (slow tension) exercises along with moving at a slow pace at whatever main activity you are going to do. The stretch exercises are used to improve flexibility and prepare the muscles, joints, and ligaments for the stress that follows from your main activity. The moving slowly increases your circulation and warms and stretches the muscles, preparing them for forceful contractions. It also gradually accelerates your heart rate preparing it to be maintained within the target heart rate zone during exercise. This warm-up period is very important for helping to reduce muscle and joint soreness.

Static stretch exercises are to be done easily and gently, avoiding bouncing and jerking. These exercises stretch the muscles beyond their normal length to the greatest possible length. It is best to stretch slowly until the muscles and connective tissue come to a point of tension that creates "stretch pain," a slight to moderate discomfort. You then hold the position for 10-30 seconds. Relax and then repeat the exercise for 3-5 times. Avoid overstretching as it can lead to injury. Some professionals advocate stretching after a few minutes of moving slowly, such as walking or easy jogging, stating that it is easier to stretch a warm muscle. The following stretch exercises give attention to stretching hamstring, calf and low back muscles so as to reduce soreness and risk of injury:

Procedure: Lie on your back, bend and bring one of your knees up to your chest, hold tight for 10 seconds. Relax and repeat with other leg 3 to 5 times with each leg. Stretches low back muscles and hip flexor.

Procedure: Lie on your back, bring both knees to the chest, hold tight for 10 seconds then straighten both legs and relax. Repeat 3-5 times. Stretches low back muscles.

Procedure: Lie on your back with your knees bent. Bring one knee toward chest then extend the leg in a straight line upward, then lock your knee in so as to keep leg straight. Hold for 10 seconds. Relax and then repeat with the other leg. Repeat 3-5 times with each leg. Stretches the hamstring muscles (muscle behind the thigh).

Procedure: Stand facing a wall about 3 feet away. In a lunge position, bring one foot forward, while keeping the back leg straight and heel flat to the floor. Allow the knee of the front leg to bend and lean forward as far as comfortably possible. Hold for 10-30 seconds. Relax and then repeat with the other leg. Repeat 3 to 5 times with each leg. As your flexibility improves, stand further away from the wall. Stretches calf muscles. (A good resource book for more stretches and information on fitness is *Being Fit—A Personal Guide* by Bud Getchell, Ph.D., John Wiley & Sons, Inc.)

The aerobic conditioning period. This period is the "heart" of your individual and family exercise program. Remember to do activities that you enjoy doing so that you will keep them up and view exercise as a lifetime activity. It is an excellent idea to do aerobic activities as a family, remembering also that everyone needs variety, especially children. The exercise prescription outlined earlier in the chapter, gives the details of this period. Remember that aerobic conditioning helps you get in shape for the games and sports that you like. Remember also to drink water before, during and after aerobic exercise, especially during hot weather.

Cool down period. This is a period of 5-10 minutes. Just as in the warm-up period, when the body is gradually prepared for the main activity by progressive increase in activity; the cool down period is used to gradually lower the level of the main activity. This is done by continuing your walking, cycling, swimming, jogging, but at a slower rate. This is done so as to allow your muscles to help in pumping the blood from your extremities back to your heart, especially the blood in your lower extremities. The cool down also helps to lower body temperature and excess norepinephrine, which is present after vigorous exercise. It is also recommended to do some stretch exercises during this period so as to prevent or reduce joint and muscle soreness. These stretches should be done following the initial slowing down period. One can also extend this period to include working on muscular strength and endurance by means of calisthenics or weight training.

NUTRITION

It is extremely important to develop a sound game plan as far as nutrition is concerned. It is necessary for establishing and maintaining a solid foundation for our bodies; one that will serve the purpose for which God created them: to be temples of the Holy Spirit. Proper nutrition provides a solid base for developing our physical, emotional, and spiritual well-being. Proper nutrition, along with exercise and rest, contributes to the development and maintenance of a vigorous, healthy body. It is well to remember that without proper nutrition, we will not have the needed energy for exercise. What you eat will determine your level of energy. It is good to think of food as human fuel; fuel that is needed for the efficient operation of our bodies. A person who eats the proper foods provides himself with the proper energy to do justice to his vocation in life and its many duties in accordance with the will of God.

There are certain principles of nutrition that are well to be considered. Parents must be models for their children in learning and incorporating these principles into their lives. Children with poor eating habits will be affected throughout the different phases of their development.

An individual or family should eat three meals a day, meals that include a variety of foods that contain carbohydrates, protein, and fat; foods that are selected from the four food groups: fruit and vegetables, bread and cereal, milk group and meat group. It is recommended to eat food that is low in fat and sugar and high in fiber.

Carbohydrates are important because they are the main source of energy for our muscles. Carbohydrates also provide glucose, the crucial energy source for the brain. They also provide needed vitamins and minerals and are high in water content and fiber, which is needed for digestion. Complex carbohydrates are found in food such as: fruits, vegetables, potatoes, pasta, corn, and whole wheat bread. It is recommended that 50 to 60 percent of your total calories be carbohydrates.

Protein is needed for repairing tissue and building up new tissue. It serves as an energy reserve when energy from carbohydrates is burned out. Food such as fish, poultry, cheese, milk, eggs, and beans are good sources of protein. It is recommended that 15 to 20 percent of your total calories be protein.

Fat is a stored source of energy that we burn during rest and light to moderate exercise. It should consist of 25 to 30 percent of our total calories.

It is important to drink 6 glasses of water a day. A basic principle for weight control consists in balancing the calories we take in with the energy or physical activity that we put out. The extra body fat is caused not so much by taking in more calories as it is in decreasing the amount of exercise we do. (An excellent resource book for nutrition, weight control and aerobic fitness is: *The Aerobic Program For Total Well-Being* by Kenneth Cooper, M.D., M.Ph., Bantam Books.)

7

Spiritual Fitness and Athletes of the Spirit

Pope John Paul II, in his homily at a Mass on May 10, 1993, in Caltanissetta, Sicily, talked about how St. Paul compared two types of athletes: athletes of sport and athletes of the faith. The Pope encouraged the young people in attendance to represent both. St. Paul ennobled exercise and sports with his own Christian perspective. He viewed everything we do, including exercise and sports, as means of giving glory to God. He viewed the body as God's creation and encouraged us to glorify God by making our bodies the shrines of His presence—just think, shrines of the Holy Spirit.

Perhaps today, we need to question ourselves on how does our physical fitness and athletic competition influence our spiritual development. Do we view physical exercise and sports as a school which develops the natural virtues that form a solid foundation for the supernatural virtues taking into mind the principle: "grace builds on nature"? The Pope has stated: "All sports can and must be formative; that is, they can and must contribute to the integral development of the "human person." [11] In his *Christian Humanism,* based on St. Thomas Aquinas' metaphysics of the human person, the Pope stresses the dignity of the human person who is made in the image and likeness of God. The Pope has proposed a renewed vision of sport based on the principle that the dignity of the human person is the goal and criterion of all sporting activity.

St. Paul, emphasizes the interior and spiritual significance of sport. In his writings, he describes the athletes in the Greek and Roman stadiums receiving a reward, a perishable wreath. He then writes about Christians receiving an imperishable reward, eternal life. St. Paul used sporting images to illustrate the life of struggle of the Christian on earth. He wrote: "You know well enough that when men run in a race, the race is for all, but the prize for one; run then; for victory" (1 Cor 9:24). And in another time, he wrote: "fight the good fight of faith" (1 Tim 6:12).

St. Paul, drawing from the concepts of the sporting culture of Greece, wrote about the importance of discipline and temperance in attaining eternal life. He wrote: "Every athlete exercises self-control in all things" (1 Cor 9:25). St. Ignatius of Antioch in his letter to Polycarp builds on this: "Be temperate, like an athlete of God; the prize is immortality and eternal life." [12] St. Paul wrote to the Corinthians, "Every athlete must keep all his appetites under control; and he does it to win a crown that fades, whereas ours is imperishable. So I do not run my course like a man in doubt of his goal; I do not fight my battle like a man who wastes his blows on the air. I buffet my own body, and make it my slave; or I, who have preached to others, may myself be rejected as worthless" (1 Cor 9:25-27).

Perhaps today we should also question ourselves on the amount of time we spend on our spiritual fitness compared to our physical fitness. The first place in man's composite being does not belong to the body, but to the soul. In the union of body and soul that forms our one nature, the principle element is the soul and not the body, which is the instrument of the soul. St. Thomas Aquinas said it well when he referred to exercise and sports as perfecting the body as an instrument of the mind and makes the mind a more refined instrument for the search and communication of truth. Winning victories of the soul is what we are to be about.

The early Father of the Church, Clement of Alexandria, clearly valued physical and spiritual fitness, but of the two, he taught that spiritual fitness is the most excellent; "that by it, the soul is made beautiful with the presence of the Holy Spirit and adornments He confers: justice, prudence, fortitude, temperance, love of the good, and modesty."[13] He taught that physical exercise cultivates symmetry of bodily members and produces a good complexion. He also taught that physical exercise is effective in maintaining health and a pleasing physical appearance.

As far as spiritual fitness is concerned, one could suppose that if one bestowed equally serious care on the interior life, as one does on exercise and sports, one would certainly be well on the road to sanctity. Perhaps it is worth remembering: "Seek ye therefore first the kingdom of God and His justice and all these things shall be added unto you" (Matt 6:33). The late eminent French Dominican theologian, Reginald Garrigou-Lagrange, O.P. in his classic book on the spiritual life, *The Three Ages of the Interior Life,* wrote: "The interior life is for all the one thing necessary. It ought to be constantly developing in our soul; more so than what we call our intellectual life, more so than our scientific, artistic or literary life." [14]

MODELS

All the saints can be called victorious athletes of the spirit. One such saint is St. Dominic, whom the Church has designated a "holy athlete of Christ." It was Pope Innocent III who called him "the invincible athlete of Christ." Pope Honorius called the members of his Order, the Dominican Order, "champions of the faith and the true light of the world." Dante called him "the athlete of Christ." St. Dominic was a man of indefatigable energy, a man of great character and depth. Joyousness sprang out of the great physical energy and immense strength of bodily endurance that he possessed. He was truly an athlete of the spirit capable of doing great things.

St. Dominic was pre-eminently a man of prayer. It was the source of his inner power and tranquility of his exterior graciousness. He was trained to look upon success as achieved not by his convincing eloquence or the logic of his argument, but by a supernatural weapon, the power of prayer. The Divine Office and the Rosary were his favorite prayers. He prayed before the Blessed Sacrament as often as he could. St. Dominic used his body in his manner of addressing God in prayer: bowing, kneeling, standing, prostrating himself, using every posture and gesture of the body. His idea of using his body in prayer was due to the rendering to God of the whole of man; every gift, or faculty of soul or body.   He was very devoted to the Mass. The New Testament was his favorite study and made the testbook of life. He constantly carried the Gospel of St. Matthew and the Epistles of St. Paul with him.

Tradition affirms that Mary herself revealed to him the Rosary in the form of mental and vocal prayer. He prayed the Rosary by contemplating on the character and virtues of Our Lord, on His mysteries—joined by saying the Our Father and Hail Marys which were noted by a string of beads. His method of preaching was to mention and develop a certain mystery of the faith and then pray the Our Father and Hail Mary divided into decades. The mysteries that were chosen at that time were chosen to combat definite error. St. Dominic used the Rosary for correcting the false dogmas of the Albigensians, who had an unnatural hatred of life. As the mysteries of the faith were gradually brought back to the minds and hearts of the people, mysteries of falsehood disappeared. The doctrine of the Incarnation, so specially commemorated in the Rosary, became then, as ever, the bulwark of the truth. St. Dominic loved praying the Rosary day and night. He knew the human heart and it is the adaptation of the Rosary to the needs of the heart that gave this form of prayer its freshness and popularity. His Rosary was his preparation for every sermon. His most famous spiritual son, St. Thomas Aquinas would one day say: "it is better to illumine than merely to shine."

Another athlete of the spirit recognized by the Church is Blessed Pier Giorgio Frassati, whose portrait appears on the cover of this book. He was beatified by Pope John Paul II on May 20, 1990. The Pope spoke of him as being a model for athletes on April 12, 1984.

Pier was open to the values of sports. He was an avid mountain climber who valued it as a means of developing character. He admired, in the pure atmosphere of the mountains, the magnificence of God. In this pristine environment of the mountains, he found it easy to contemplate, seeing God reflected in His creation. This led him to lift up his mind and heart to God in a spirit of prayer, offering praise and gratitude to God. He was also an able skier, never missing making a visit to the Blessed Sacrament after skiing. He was very devoted to the Mass, attending it and receiving Communion everyday. He had a practice of making frequent visits to the Blessed Sacrament.

He was also very fond of swimming, rowing and bicycle riding. He was a man of deep prayer, who recognized the chief ends of prayer: adoration, reparation, thanksgiving and petition. He loved praying the Rosary. He prayed the Rosary three times a day after he became a member of the Third Order of St. Dominic. He treasured the Rosary, which, in a sense, epitomizes Dominican spirituality; offering a way of meditating, pondering and proclaiming the truths of faith expressed in the form of praise.

His infectious smile and joy of living attracted followers. He was born to give and not just to live for himself. He loved the poor; he passed through their midst doing good to them. His fondness for the epistles of St. Paul sparked his zeal for fraternal charity. At graduation from the Polytechnic University in Turin, Italy, he was given a choice of money or a car by his father; he chose the money and gave it to the poor. His ambition after graduation was to marry and to emigrate, perhaps to America, as a lay apostle.

Pier was interested in the social teachings of the Catholic Church. He gave time and money to help establish a Catholic daily newspaper, *Momento*, which was based on the principles of the papal social encyclical *Rerum Novarum*. He desired that the social teachings of the Catholic Church would influence the culture of his time.

Polio struck Blessed Pier at the age of 24. He had no fear of death. He said: "I think the day of my death will be the happiest day of my life." He died with a smile on his face and a Rosary in his hand.

PRESCRIPTION FOR SPIRITUAL FITNESS

Athletes and coaches are familiar with having a game plan for their upcoming contest. They know what it takes to prepare themselves for putting forth their best effort in order to win. The game plan involves using the best strategy, using the best plays from the playbook that will produce the advantage, the winning edge.

Those who pursue spiritual fitness, athletes of the spirit, are like athletes of the field; loyal to the training rules and training aids; not allowing tiredness nor any obstacle to halt them until their goal is reached, eternal life with God. They are aware that they need to train, to develop a spirituality so that they can be builders of the civilization of love here on earth and to save their soul and be united with God in heaven for eternity. They know that the self-discipline developed through physical fitness and sports will help them develop a proper mindset, a proper attitude in striving for eternal life with God. Athletes of the spirit recognize the need for a game plan that includes self-denial and self-mastery in the moral life so as to gain the imperishable reward. They know that the Christian life demands systematic spiritual training since the Christian "like every athlete exercises self-control in all things" (1 Cor 9:25).

Athletes of the spirit are like athletes of sport who display persistence in resisting exhaustion, knowing that they must develop the perseverance of a marathon runner; knowing that Jesus said: "By patient endurance you will save your lives" (Luke 21:19). These athletes of the spirit know that the spiritual life demands patience, not expecting it to be easy; for them physical fitness and sports have tempered the character and have formed a will as hard as steel so that they can say with St. Paul: "I buffet my body and make it my slave" (1 Cor 9:27), and so practice mortification and with God's grace, practice the virtues.

Athletes of sport look to their instructors, their coaches for supplying them with a game plan, a strategy, a set of plays from the playbook that will give them an advantage, that will put them into a position to be victorious. With their eyes set on victory, they submit to the instruction and discipline of the coach.

Athletes of the spirit look to the Catholic Church and to the Vicar of Christ, John Paul II for their instruction, for their game plan; a strategy that will put them into a position to be victorious in gaining eternal life with God. God who wants all men to be saved and to know the truth (1 Tim 2:4), has given mankind the Catholic Church to teach man the light of the truth, which leads to eternal life. God has entrusted to the Catholic Church the correct interpretation of the divinely revealed truth on man's redemption and his inheritance of eternal life. In Karol Wojtyla's (Pope John Paul II) book, *The Way to Christ*, he mentions that: "The Church was organized from within by Christ himself, who said to Peter: "You are Peter, and on this rock I will build my church, and the powers of death shall not prevail against it. I will give you the keys of the kingdom of heaven, and whatever you bind on earth, shall be bound in heaven, and whatever you loose on earth, shall be loosed in heaven" (Matt 16:16-18). [14]   In these words, we see Peter and every successor of his, to be the rock on which the Catholic Church is built, the one who is to be strong and faithful, the one to give stability to Christ's Church.

John Paul II, the successor of Peter, is the rock on which the Church of our time is built. The athlete of the spirit looks to the Catholic Church and John Paul II as their instructors. For the athlete of the spirit to cross the finish line and be victorious in receiving the imperishable prize that God offers them, they need to submit to the teachings of the Catholic Church and John Paul II, just as the athlete of sport needs to submit to the instructions of their coach in order to carry off the victory.

TRAINING AIDS

The competition today for the athlete of the spirit is secular humanism; a viewpoint that sees nature as self-sufficient and human life as the only life there is. It denies the existence of God, His revelation, supernatural life and eternal life with God. In order for the athlete of the spirit to be spiritually strong against this foe, he must make use of the training aids the Church offers. They are: 1) instruction for the renewal of the mind, 2) prayer, 3) the sacraments.

INSTRUCTION FOR THE RENEWAL OF THE MIND

St. Paul in his letter to the Romans stated: "Do not be conformed to this world but be transformed by the renewal of your mind" (Rom 12:2). The Church offers the Sacred Scriptures, especially the Gospels, in helping us renew our minds. The Second Vatican Council refers to the Gospels as "the source of all saving truth and moral teaching" (*Dei Verbum*, n.7). The Church also offers her athletes of the spirit the new *Catechism of the Catholic Church*, the newest compendium of Catholic doctrine; a statement of the Church's faith and of Catholic doctrine. The Pope views this new Catechism as intended for all the faithful who wish to deepen their knowledge of the unfathomable riches of salvation. The new Catechism is offered to all who want to know what the Catholic Church believes. John Paul II said: "It is a gift which the Heavenly Father grants to His children offering them through this Catechism the possibility of knowing Him better in the light of the spirit."

Athletes of the spirit also have the opportunity of renewing their minds by reading the encyclical letters and apostolic exhortations of Pope John Paul II. The Pope's newest Encyclical Letter *The Splendor of Truth* is a marvelous work which is meant to be a companion to the new *Catechism of the Catholic Church*. It is a splendid reflection on the principles of the moral life. It reaffirms the dignity and greatness of the human person, created in God's image; it sets forth the concept of freedom and how it is related to Jesus' words: "The Truth will make you free." The social teachings of the Church that are contained in John Paul's encyclicals are indispensable for the athlete of the spirit in understanding the social, economic, political, and cultural aspects of their life.

The guiding principle of the Church's social teaching is the correct view of the human person and his unique value, being created in the image and likeness of God. Three of John Paul's encyclicals that deal with the social teachings of the Church are: *On Human Work, On Social*

Concern, and *On the Hundredth Anniversary of Rerum Novarum.* An excellent work of John Paul's that deals with the true nature of man is his first Encyclical Letter *The Redeemer of Man.*

The Church also offers her athletes of the spirit a proper understanding and vision of marriage, human sexuality and family life. Pope Paul VI's Encyclical Letter *Humantae Vitae* represents a call to reverence God's vision of marriage and human sexuality. John Paul's Apostolic Exhortation *The Role of the Christian Family in the Modern World* is also an excellent work, for the proper understanding of God's plan for marriage and the family. Excellent companions to this work would be John Paul's Apostolic Exhortation *Guardian of the Redeemer,* a work on St. Joseph, and his Apostolic Letter *On the Dignity and Vocation of Woman.* An excellent summary of John Paul's theology of the body, of his teachings on sexuality, marriage and the family is the book, *Covenant of Love.* (Available from Ignatius Press, San Franciso. Papal encyclicals are available from St. Paul Books and Media, Boston.)

PRAYER

The athlete of sport uses exercise and nutrition to build up strength for the game on the field. The athlete of the spirit uses prayer to build up spiritual strength for the game of life and for achieving the final reward of eternal life with God. Prayer is the simplest and most widely practiced way of obtaining grace; grace needed to lead to victory over sin and its forces; grace to keep us close to God and to inwardly transform us; grace needed to strengthen the work of conscience in directing us to the true and good.

St. John Damascene defines prayer as "the lifting up of the mind and heart to God." St. Augustine wrote that to love and possess God in the everlasting security of eternal life should be the final object of all our prayers. St. Thomas Aquinas, universal teacher of the Church, reminds us that prayer should be made with: confidence, rectitude, order, devoutness, and humility. Through his teachings, we learn that prayer benefits us in three ways: it remedies evils, it obtains that which we desire, and establishes friendship with God. (An excellent book on prayer written by St. Thomas Aquinas is *The Three Greatest Prayers*, Sophia Press.)

Prayer is truly a gift from God. St. Francis de Sales in his classic, *The Introduction to the Devout Life*, states: "Prayer places our intellect in the brilliance of God's light and exposes our will to the warmth of his heavenly love, nothing else so effectly purifies our intellect of ignorance and our will of depraved affections." [16] As far as mental prayer is concerned, this great saint, a true instructor in spiritual skills, advises us that the life and death of Jesus is the most fitting and profitable subject that can be chosen for our ordinary meditations. He advises that vocal prayer, such as the Our Father or Hail Mary, be said with feeling and not said quickly and hurriedly. Vocal and mental prayer includes acts of adoration, thanksgiving, petition and reparation. The prayer of petition acknowledges the truth that God alone is the source of all good things.

We see on television the Nike commercial with the words: "Life is short—play hard"; would not the saying: "Life is short—pray hard" be more fitting for the athlete of the spirit? We also see football teams on television use the desperation pass called the "Hail Mary pass", for a last-resort, seconds-to-go play; whereas, the athlete of the spirit hears the Church teach us to pray continually and not just in time of urgent need or emergency.

Though we are called to private prayer, we are also called to prayer with others. Jesus said: "Again I say to you—if two of you agree on earth about anything they ask, it will be done for them by my Father in heaven. For when two or three are gathered in my name, there am I in the midst of them." Pope John Paul II urges family prayer, especially the family Rosary. In his Apostolic Exhortation *The Role of the Christian Family in the Modern World*, he states: "The dignity and responsibility of the Christian family as the domestic Church can be achieved only with God's unceasing aid, which will surely be granted if it is humbly and trustingly petitioned in prayer."[17] He also stated in the same work: "Only by praying together with their children can a father and mother penetrate the innermost depths of their children's hearts and leave an impression that the future events in their lives will not be able to efface."[18]

John Paul II, a man of deep prayer, sees work as taking up most of our time. But he believes that all activities should be rooted in prayer as though in a spiritual soil and that the depth of this soil must not be too thin. He sees his own thoughts and words pass through prayer; conforming to the Thomistic principle—hand on to others the fruits of your prayer.

It is very beneficial and fitting for the athlete of the spirit to pray to the Holy Spirit for enlightenment and guidance and to seek His help in knowing what to pray for. In his first Encyclical Letter *The Redeemer of Man*, John Paul II refers to the prayer: "Come, Holy Spirit!" Come! Come! "Heal our wounds, our strength renew; On our dryness pour your dew; Wash the stains of guilt away; Bend the stubborn heart and will; Melt the frozen, warm the chill; Guide the steps that go astray."[19] He refers to this appeal to the Holy Spirit as being a means of obtaining the Holy Spirit and also as an answer to all the "materialisms" of our age. In his new Encyclical Letter *The Splendor of Truth*, the Pope wrote: "The Spirit of Jesus, received by the humble and docile heart of the believer, brings about the flourishing of Christian moral life and the witness of holiness amid the great variety of vocations, gifts, responsibilities, conditions, and life situations."[20] An excellent work which helps in developing a better knowledge of and devotion to the Holy Spirit is John Paul's Encyclical Letter *On the Holy Spirit in the Life of the Church and the World.* This work can definitely help the athlete of the spirit in preparing, in the power of the Holy Spirit, for the year 2,000; the great Jubilee which will mark the passage from the second to the third Christian Millennium.

The Rosary is the most popular devotional prayer. Many popes have praised the Rosary as a spiritual training school, where people whose muscles of the spirit have grown flabby and atrophied, can slowly and normally win back the strength required to come off victoriously in the great battle of life. Pope Paul VI, in his Apostolic Exhortation *For the Right Ordering and Development of Devotion to the Blessed Virgin Mary*, devoted a section of it to the Rosary. He described the Rosary as "the compendium of the entire Gospel."

The Rosary has all the necessary ingredients of prayer. John Paul II teaches that: "the Rosary is a prayer "concerning Mary" united with Christ in His salvific mission. At the same time it is a prayer "to Mary"…our best mediatrix with her Son. Finally, it is a prayer that in a special way we recite "with Mary" as the Apostles in the

Upper Room prayed with her, preparing themselves to receive the Holy Spirit."[21] John Paul II wrote a marvelous encyclical letter on Mary called *Mother of the Redeemer*, which is highly recommended for the athlete of the spirit who wishes to develop a filial relationship with Mary, his spiritual mother.

Mary is the most perfect model of Christian contemplation. Praying the Rosary with Mary, she will enlighten our mind and teach us the meaning of each of the fifteen mysteries. The athlete of the spirit will then pray like Mary did, when he ponders over the mysteries that Mary pondered on during her life on earth and which she continues to do in heaven. Mary appeared at Fatima, Portugal, in 1917, and asked that the Rosary be prayed everyday. She has promised many graces and blessings for those who pray the Rosary. John Cassian, a spiritual writer in the 4th century, wrote of the athlete of the spirit partaking in an Olympic struggle against their vices. One of Mary's promises to those who pray the Rosary, is that it will destroy vice and decrease sin. (Excellent books on the Rosary are: *Secrets of the Rosary*, by St. Louis de Montfort, Montfort Publications, Bay Shore, N.Y. and *The Rosary: The Little Summa*, Aquinas Press.)

THE SACRAMENTS

Another power-source for the athlete of the spirit is the sacraments. Jesus established in the Catholic Church the seven sacraments in order to give to those who receive them a share in the grace which He won for each person through His passion, death and resurrection. The Second Vatican Council referred to the purpose of the sacraments as being: to sanctify men, to build up the Body of Christ and give worship to God.

The athlete of the spirit has the opportunity to receive the sacraments of the Eucharist and Penance frequently. The Church encourages her members to unite themselves more closely to Christ through these sacraments. St. Thomas Aquinas wrote of these two sacraments in terms of the life of the spirit having a certain similarity to the life of the body:

THE EUCHARIST: In the life of the body, man requires food so that his life may be preserved and sustained; so also in the life of the spirit, after being fortified, he requires spiritual food, which is Christ's body: "Unless you shall eat of the flesh of the Son of Man, and drink of His blood, you shall not have life in you" (John 6:54). The Second Vatican Council described the Mass as "the primary and indispensable source from which the faithful are to derive the true Christian spirit" (Constitution on the Sacred Liturgy, n.4). It also taught that "the Eucharist is the source and summit of Christian life" (n.4).

PENANCE: In the life of the body, a man is sometimes sick, and unless he takes medicine, he will die. Likewise, in the life of the spirit, a man is sick on account of sin; thus, he needs medicine that he may be restored to health. This grace is bestowed in the Sacrament of Penance. The Church recommends frequent confession for advancement in the path of virtue, for true knowledge of ourselves, for bad habits to be uprooted, for our conscience to be purified and our will strengthened. Pope John Paul II wrote an excellent apostolic exhortation on Penance called *On Reconciliation and Penance.*

In conclusion, the two main power sources for the athlete of the spirit are prayer and the sacraments. Without the aid of grace, a person cannot do anything good. The sacraments, meritorious good works and prayer are powerful means of obtaining the grace necessary for the athlete of the spirit to receive the crown; the imperishable reward of union and possession of God in heaven.

About the Author

Robert Feeney is a native of Alexandria, Virginia. He holds a Bachelor of Arts degree in Physical Education from Carroll College in Helena, Montana, and a Master of Science degree in Physical Education from the University of Dayton. He has taught physical education on the university, high school and grade school levels. He is a member of the Third Order of St. Dominic and author of the books *Mother of the Americas* and *The Rosary: The Little Summa.*

Notes

[1] Earle Zeigler, Ph.D., *History of Sport and Physical Education to 1900,* Stipes Publishing Co., Champaign, IL, 1973, p. 191.

[2] Donna Miller, Kathryn Russell, *Sport: a Contemporary View*, Lea & Febiger, Philadelphia, PA, 1971, p. 91.

[3] A. G. Sertillanges, O.P., *The Intellectual Life*, Christian Classics, Westminister, MD, 1980, p. 34-35

[4] Donna Miller, Ph.D., *The Philosophic Process in Physical Education,* Lea and Febiger, Philadelphia, PA, 1977, p. 145.

[5] Ibid., p. 147

[6] Ibid., p. 196

[7] Kenneth Cooper, M.D., *The Aerobic Way,* M. Evans & Co., Inc., New York, N.Y., 1977, p.. 183.

[8] Ronald M. Lawrence, M.D., Ph.D., *Going the Distance*, Jeremy P. Tarcher, Inc., Los Angeles, CA, 1987, p.18.

[9] Ibid., p. 18

[10] Michael Pollock, Jack Wilmore, and Samuel Fox, *Health and Fitness through Physical Activity*, John Wiley & Son, New York, N.Y., 1978.

[11] *L'Osservatore Romano* (Vatican City, Jan 3-10, 1983), p. 4.

[12] *The Apostolic Fathers,* CIMA Publishing, N.Y., 1947, p. 125.

[13] *Fathers of the Church, Inc.,* N.Y., 1954, p. 249

[14] Reginald Garrogou-Lagrange, O.P., *The Three Ages of the Interior Life,* Benziger, New York, N.Y., 1938, p.1.

[15] Karol Wojtyla, *The Way to Christ,* Harper & Row, San Francisco, 1984, p. 74.

[16] St. Francis de Sales, *The Introduction to the Devout Life,* Image Books, Garden City, N.Y., 1972, p. 81.

[17] *The Role of the Christian Family in the Modern World,* Pope John Paul II, Daughters of St. Paul, Boston, MA, 1981, p. 88.

[18] Ibid., p. 89.

[19] Pope John Paul II, *The Redeemer of Man,* U. S. Catholic Conference, Washington, D.C., 1979, p. 71.

[20] Pope John Paul II, *The Splendor of Truth,* Daughters of St. Paul, Boston, MA, 1993, p. 130.

[21] Pope John Paul II, *A Year With Mary,* Catholic Books Publishing Co., New York, N.Y., 1986, p. 220.

Bibliography

Bailey, Covert. *The New Fit or Fat*. Boston, MA: Houghton Miffin Co., 1991.

Cooper, Kenneth, M.D., M.Ph. *Aerobics*. N.Y., New York: M. Evans & Co., 1968.

Cooper, Kenneth, M.D., M.Ph. *Kid Fitness*. N.Y., New York: Bantam Books, 1991.

Cooper, Kenneth, M.D., M.Ph. *The Aerobics Program for Total Well-Being*. N.Y., New York: Bantam Books, 1982.

Cooper, Kenneth, M.D., M.Ph. *The Aerobics Way*. N.Y., New York: Bantam Books, 1978.

de Vries, Herbert A. *Fitness After 50*. N.Y., N.Y: Charles Scribner's & Sons, 1982.

Getchell, Bud, Ph.D. *Physical Fitness: A Way of Life*. N.Y., N.Y: John Wiley & Sons, Inc., 1979.

Getchell, Bud, Ph.D. *Being Fit—A Personal Guide*. N.Y., N.Y: John Wiley & Sons, 1982.

Glover, Bob & Shepherd, Jack. *The Family Fitness Handbook*. Penguin Books, 1989.

Lawrence, Ronald, M.D., Ph.D. *Going the Distance.* Los Angeles, CA: Jeremy P. Tarcher, Inc., 1987.

L'Osservatore Romano. Vatican City: 1979-87.

Miller, David & Allen, T. Earl. *Fitness—A Lifetime Commitment.* N.Y., N.Y: MacMillian Pub. Co., 1990.

Monks of Solesmes. *The Human Body.* Boston: The Daughters of Saint Paul, 1960.

Pollock, Michael, Wilmore, Jack, Fox, Samuel. *Health & Fitness Through Physical Activity.* N.Y., N.Y: John Wiley & Sons, 1978.

Rippe, James, M. D. *The Sports Performance Factors.* N.Y., N.Y: Putnam Publishing, Co., 1986.

Steinhaus, Authur Ph.D. *Toward an Understanding of Health & Physical Education.* Dubuque, IA: Wm. C. Brown, Co., 1963.

Van Aaken, Ernst, M.D. *The Van Aaken Method.* Mountain View, CA: World Publication, 1976.

Vitale, Frank. *Individualized Fitness Programs.* Englewood Cliffs, N.J: Prentice Hall, Inc., 1973.

Wilmore, Jack, Ph.D. *Sensible Fitness.* Champaign, IL: Leisure Press, 1986.